Cistercian Studies Series: Number One Hundred Seventy-Seven

Maxims
Stephen of Muret

MAXIMS

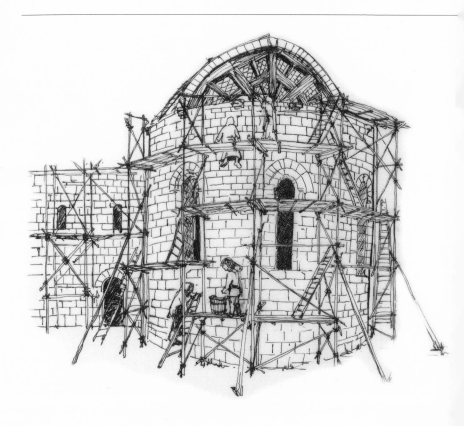

STEPHEN *of* MURET

Translation by DEBORAH VAN DOEL OCD

Preface by DOM JEAN BECQUET OSB

Introduction by CAROLE HUTCHISON

Illustrations by KATE DOUGLAS

Edited by MAUREEN M. O'BRIEN

CISTERCIAN PUBLICATIONS   Kalamazoo, Michigan 2002

This translation has been made from
Dom Jean Becquet, osb, ed., *Liber de Doctrina*
in *Corpus Christianorum Continuatio Mediaevalis*, VIII
(Turnhout, Belgium: 1968).

The work of Cistercian Publications
is made possible in part by support from Western Michigan University
to The Institute of Cistercian Studies

Available from

Cistercian Publications
Editorial Offices and Customer Service
Institute of Cistercian Studies
Western Michigan University
Kalamazoo, MI 49008

British and European Customer Service
97 Loughborough Road
Thringstone, Coalville, Leic. LE67 8LZQ

http://www.spencerabbey.org/cistpub/

Typeset by Gale Akins in *Monotype Spectrum*
Humble Hills Press
350 East Michigan Ave., Suite 407
Kalamazoo, MI 49007-3800

PRINTED IN THE UNITED STATES OF AMERICA

ISBN 0-87907-677-1 (hc)
0-87907-777-8 (pb)

TABLE OF CONTENTS

PREFACE

It is no coincidence that the first translation of the *Maxims* of Stephen of Muret was produced by Adrien Baillet at the very beginning of the seventeenth century. An odd pastime for a scholar, one might say, but considering that mysticism experienced something of a revival at the dawn of the Enlightenment, why would not such a penetrating spirit feel the seductive and edifying power of this text which is so redolent of the Gospel? Even so, the *Maxims* were bound to suffer from the dereliction into which history has brought grandmontine institutions generally. Only at the end of our century has there appeared an Italian, and now this English, translation to complement the new French edition.

Doubtless there are two very different factors which have contributed to this renewal of interest. On the one hand, Church historians since Johann von Walter, Augustin Flich, and many others have concentrated on the roots of the eleventh- and twelfth-century reform of religious life in the Latin West, a time when the understanding of primitive christian monasticism was greatly deepened. On the other hand, the cultural upheavals in the West after World War II have cast doubt on certain medieval modes of life which were too readily adopted as a result of the tridentine systematization. The present necessity for authentic renewal is thus best met by a stripping-down of the documentation that can provide and make widely available (with gratitude here to Abbé Migne!) the supports needed for fresh research.

'*Habent sua fata libri.*' How will christian religious of the twenty-first century hold on to Stephen of Muret's *Maxims* in the face of the wealth of experience offered by India and the Far East? We cannot as yet say, but the translation of these maxims into those major languages still impregnated with Latin may well promote new buds and shoots on the tree of western spirituality.

J. Becquet osb
Ligugé

INTRODUCTION

These *Maxims* are the spiritual teachings of Saint Stephen of Muret that he imparted to a group of followers who joined him in his hermitage at Muret between the years 1075 and his death in 1124. This small community turned out to be the nucleus of a very unusual religious order of hermit monks. The Order of Grandmont, as it was eventually known, was named after the small hamlet of Grandmont, twelve miles to the north of Limoges where the mother house was established in 1125. Although the Grandmontines were not fully constituted until some considerable time after Stephen's death, his sons always regarded him as their founder and certainly it was his ideas which inspired their way of life.

What little is actually known about Stephen has been confused by subjective biographies and pious legends. Tradition has it that he was educated in Italy by the archbishop of Benevento in the schools of that city and that he subsequently held ecclesiastical office in Rome before returning to his native France to dedicate his life to God as a solitary. The *Vita Stephani* [1] insists that he was or-

---

1. *Vita Venerabilis Viri Stephani Muretensis,* SG, 124. Abbreviation 'SG' refers to: *Scriptores Ordinis Grandimontensis in Corpus Christianorum Continuatio Mediaevalis,* VIII, edited by Dom Jean Becquet (Turnhout, Belgium: 1968).

dained a deacon but that he refused priestly ordination. It also makes much of a youthful sojourn with a group of eastern monks who had settled in Calabria and who were to exercise a great influence over his vocation and teaching, but it fails to identify the brethren concerned. All we can know for certain about Stephen is that sometime during the 1070's he built himself a hermit's cell in the forest of Muret, and remained there until his death. It is unlikely that he ever set eyes on Grandmont even though it is only a few miles distant from the site of his hermitage.

In due course, others who were desirous of imitating his example and dedicating their lives to God as solitaries joined Stephen. With them he shared his spiritual riches in the manner of the apophthegmatic teaching of the Desert Fathers. Stephen personally never wrote anything down. His *Thoughts,* or *Maxims,* as they came to be known, were orally transmitted by his disciples.

It was another Stephen, Stephen Liciac, who, when he became fourth prior of Grandmont in 1139, was responsible for compiling the teachings and sayings of Stephen of Muret into the *Liber de Doctrina.*[2] He also formulated the *Rule of Grandmont*[3] which received the approbation of Pope Adrian IV in 1156. While this work draws from Stephen of Muret's personal notions concerning the religious life, it is essentially the formal embodiment of a code of conduct for life in community and as such is a document intended strictly for religious. The *Maxims* themselves have a far wider appeal. The chief compiler of the work was Stephen's closest companion, Hugh Lacerta whose *Vita*[4] tells us was a knight and former

2. Dom Jean Becquet, ed., *Liber de Doctrina,* SG, 3ff.
3. *Regula Venerabilis Viri Stephani Muretensis,* SG, 65-99. The text of the so called *Rule of Stephen of Muret* is generally referred to as the *Rule of Grandmont.*
4. *Vita Hugonis Lacerta,* SG, 172.

crusader before he joined Stephen at Muret as one of the *viri illiterati*; lay brethren, unschooled in Latin. What Hugh and his companions may have lacked in linguistic skills was more than compensated for by the acuteness of their combined memory that rescued this spiritual treasure from sinking into oblivion. In the absence of any reliable documentary evidence concerning Stephen of Muret it is only in his *Maxims* that we are able to find a reflection of that spiritual countenance which attracted generations of hermit monks into the wilderness to dedicate themselves to a life based wholly on the Gospel Rule of Christ.

It was not only hermits, however, who were to be found at Muret. As the fame of his holiness spread, Stephen was subjected to a constant stream of visitors all eagerly seeking his spiritual direction. This was obviously not what Stephen had expected when he embraced the life of the hermitage. He could have taken to his heels and sought an alternative, even more hidden site in which to pursue his personal vocation. Instead, he accepted the responsibility for novices as well as the influx of casual visitors as the will of God. 'He received all visitors', the Prologue to the *Rule of Grandmont* relates, 'as the father of a family.' And it was with love that he unselfishly sacrificed his own preference for intimacy with God and instead dedicated a large part of his time to counseling them. 'He drew daily from his own treasury of riches those jewels he had himself proved by long and pious perseverance.'[5]

These jewels are not lengthy, scholarly treatises, rather they are short, pithy, easily digestible comments and aphorisms intended

---

5. The actual observation concerning Stephen's manner of counseling contained in the Prologue to the *Rule* is: '*Doctus quippe ille paterfamilias cotidie coram eis proferebat de thesauro suo nova et vetera, quos non auditores tantum veram etiam praeceptorum Dei factores longa piae devotionis perseverantia probaverate*'(SG, 65).

to strike at the heart and be easily committed to memory by ordinary folk. The discourses, it is true, are of varying lengths, some only two or three lines, others, more than a page. Prior Liciac was probably responsible for grouping the *Maxims* by subject matter under appropriate headings.

The Prologue highlights the essential theme that pervades the entire work: 'There is no other Rule but the Gospel of Christ'. To live, as did the apostles following the teaching of Christ to the letter, this is the essence of Stephen's vocation. In the introduction to the *Maxims*, Stephen qualifies this statement with a certain degree of polemic directed at religious rules which substitute too much human wisdom for the simple and direct instruction of the New Testament which is the only 'way' that leads to complete unity between fellow Christians and Christ their guide, that is, the 'body of Christ' which Saint Paul exhorts in his epistle to the Ephesians.[6] Stephen's reflections are directed primarily toward a group whom, if not professed monks in the strict sense, were nevertheless dedicated to some form of religious life. Therefore, the first section of the *Maxims* is inevitably concerned with advice about entry into the religious state, that is, the sort of temptations that the novice may encounter and how best he may overcome them. Gradually the instruction becomes more generalized and is appropriate for all who desire to follow Christ in whatever walk of life. From this we may assume that visitors who, according to the *Vita,* 'were always welcome at Muret', were at times party to these conferences. In the Prologue Stephen observes: 'Any Christians who have come together to live as one can claim the right to be called monks, even if the name is more particularly given to those who, like the apostles, kept a greater distance from the business of the world, giving their minds to the thought of God alone'.

6. Ep 4:13.

Christ himself, he continues, instituted the religious life in the very first sermon he preached and, 'Blessed are the poor in spirit',[7] are the words with which he commenced his Rule. All other rules are 'simply streams from the same source'. The Gospel is the 'Rule of Rules' and those who adhere to it are members of the Order of Jesus Christ. Christian community life is about loving, helping, and sharing. Each member has an individual place to occupy and a task to perform. Stephen recognized no distinction between contemplative and worker, the Marthas and the Marys. In this he was laying the foundations for a very unusual religious order; one in which there would be total equality between the choir monks and lay brethren. All lived together sharing the same choir, refectory, and dormitory. Muret at the outset was truly in accordance with the apostolic tradition: brothers having all things in common.[8] Human nature being what it is, such a system was destined to fail and before a century had lapsed quarreling erupted between the two groups of brethren. The sad but inevitable outcome was that the Order of Grandmont was reconstituted in 1317 along more conservative religious lines; nevertheless, Stephen's practice of Christ's teaching on equality at least survived as an ideal.

Christ's words to the rich young man in Matthew's Gospel[9] are a direct call to the religious life. In company with this young man do we not all feel sadness as we read this narrative knowing full well that we likewise are unable or unwilling to sacrifice our freedom, our possessions, and ourselves? Christ does not soften the blow; he had no words of consolation for the saddened young man as he went on his way. Stephen is somewhat gentler on us weaker mor-

7. Mt 5:3.
8. Ac 2:44.
9. Mt 19:21.

tals, but a lot tougher on those who do accept Christ's invitation. He reiterates such Gospel paradoxes as: 'losing so as to find life' and 'dying so as to live', but he warns that those who live a monastic life have not the same temptations to grapple with as those they would have in the world. Therefore, those who fall within the monastery will fall much farther than those outside.

Gradually we become aware that Stephen is directing his thoughts to people and matters outside the hermit enclave. In paragraph sixty, for example, he dwells strikingly, and surely unnecessarily for a group of religious brethren, on the subject of warfare: 'Pillaging is a greater sin than is simple thieving, for the first has a viler pride behind it'. A fifteenth century French translation of the *Speculum Maius*, the vast encyclopedia of the Middle Ages compiled by Vincent de Beauvais around 1250, contains a miniature which shows Stephen preaching in his hermitage. In it, he is about to be visited by three rough looking characters all armed to the teeth. A friend of the hermits hastens to warn them of the approaching danger. The image of brigands and their consequent reform following an encounter with a 'holy man of God', has many parallels in medieval hagiographies. Nevertheless it is quite conceivable that a hermitage in a forest, only twelve miles from a major city, would have afforded concealment for outlaws, brigands, and the discharged mercenaries who frequently roamed the countryside at this time. That Stephen's thought about pillaging seems more suited to a military chaplain than the spiritual director of a group of hermits, suggests that characters such as these may well have found a welcome within the enclosure at Muret. Certainly in the conclusion to the *Vita,* we are told that Stephen was insistent that social outcasts such as prostitutes and actors should be received with gentleness and kindness and that food and other necessities

XV

should be offered to them before spiritual counsel.[10]

Stephen's thoughts on prayer are equally not exclusive to religious. Those of us who find prayer difficult, are too easily distracted or simply too lazy, may take comfort from the words he puts into the mouth of Christ and which echo those spoken by him in the Gospel: 'Why rely on your own words when you have me? I am still here with you carrying out my duties on your behalf'.[11]

The instruction on the sort of attitude to adopt for prayer—whether to stand, kneel, raise our arms, or join our hands—is eminently practical. God, according to Stephen, does not wish us to focus on our discomfort rather than on him, so, when we pray privately, we should choose the position which suits each of us and the one which will increase our feelings of love for God. Such advice has a very modern ring, and is poles apart from the medieval conception of a saint, all mortification and hairshirts.

While Stephen's Maxims were intended as practical aids to spiritual growth, they also represent the outpourings of a soul suffused with the love of God. In treating of sin and evil, the tone is prosaic and direct: 'The wicked have no one to blame but themselves for the shame and disgrace they must bear'.[12] How contrastingly beautiful and poetic are the passages where he revels in the sheer, utter bliss that closeness with God can bring:

10. *Conclusio Vitae Stephani Muretensis*, SG, 324.
11. *Maxims*, Chapter Eighty: cf. Mt 28:20.
12. *Maxims*, Chapter Ninety-Nine.

Do you find your delight in God?
That is because he delights in you.
Can you rest quiet in him?
That is because God can take rest in you.[13]

This, the first English translation of the *Maxims* of Stephen of Muret by Sister Deborah van Doel, OCD, follows the critical edition of Dom Jean Becquet, OSB.[14] Latin purists may well disapprove of some of the liberties which have been taken with the Latin text, the colloquial, familiar style which has been adopted. In defense of this it must be said that Stephen was no Saint Bernard preaching to educated choir monks. He was a simple hermit, sharing his spiritual wisdom with his fellow hermits and lay folk. We can be as certain as it is possible to be that Stephen communicated his teaching in the vernacular. Hugh Lacerta was almost certainly unlettered and it was the educated prior Stephen Liciac who translated his remembrances into the Latin text that was to form the basis for the *Rule of Grandmont*.

The Order of Grandmont was dissolved in 1772 at the instigation of a french royal commission which was convened to inquire into the affairs of religious communities. The Grandmontines were targeted for extinction ostensibly because they were too few in number to justify their continuing as an independent Order. In reality, however, it was to justify the greed of bishops anxious to get their hands on grandmontine lands and revenues. Although this little known religious order is no more, it has given us two great legacies: the *Maxims* of its founder and its unique style of architecture.

All the surviving grandmontine churches are built to a uniform

14. *Maxims,* Chapter Ninety-Nine.
15. *Liber de Doctrina,* SG, 3ff.

plan with a tunnel-vaulted nave terminating in an apse that is slightly broader. Anyone who visits one of these churches in the early morning hours cannot fail to be moved by something of the intense spiritual experience that, each day, must have gladdened the hearts of the original occupants. For, at this time, the eyes are irresistibly drawn towards the sanctuary as the first ray of light penetrates the northernmost window of the apsidal triplet. It is like a theatrical spotlight which streams in to strike the wall with a circle of pure, white light. As the morning wears on, the light increases as the rays penetrate all three apertures. Eventually, from the still shadowy nave, the sanctuary appears transformed by an intense concentration of brilliant, almost blinding, light: 'the light from on high hath visited us; to enlighten them that sit in darkness and in the shadow of death; to direct our feet into the way of peace'.[15]

There is no space here to give further details of the very unusual and beautiful monasteries of the Order of Grandmont but it was thought appropriate to illustrate this translation of the *Maxims*, the spiritual foundation of the Order, with a series of drawings which reveal something of the corresponding material legacy: the unusual style of architecture which was specifically engineered for small communities of hermit monks who believed, as did their founder that: 'Religious life is grace, justice, and security. And [that] when God draws anyone to it, he has brought such a one back to Paradise.'[16]

15. Lk 1:19.
16. *Maxims*, Chapter Two.

MAXIMS
STEPHEN *of* MURET

PROLOGUE

It is the duty—and therefore a reliable and powerful means toward salvation—for those faithful servants whom the Lord has placed over his household,[1] to urge their disciples on lest they fall away from their conscientious habits. And while a shepherd's loving concern never seeks personal gain,[2] still, the disciples need always pay close attention to the behavior of a good leader, who like Saint Paul can say, 'I beg you to copy me'.[3] Of all the tangible things by which the Lord makes plain his truth, human speech and behavior are superior to any, and whoever assists the faithful by such means will deserve their warmest affection. Surely this is something that we, the brethren of Grandmont, can say about Stephen, the first and most revered shepherd of our communities.

However long ago it has been since we turned toward the light of faith, and advanced along the path of virtue, we will never go the whole distance of that straight path unless there is someone to lead us who knows how to avoid all the dangerous wrong turnings along the way. Other-

3

wise we would be like sheep that will not quit their accus-
tomed scrubland, refusing to follow the shepherd who
longs to take them onto rich pastures.[4] In the end these
will either be devoured by the wolf, or wasted, faint and
bleating in their confusion, they are left outside the
sheepfold. New walls will stand strong only when they have
been strictly aligned upon the foundations put down by
the master builder. So, most beloved brothers, let it be
our highest joy—after the gift of faith—to have had a good
shepherd to whose wonderful accomplishments we can
always look, and unfailingly hold. For what other wealth
have we to draw upon to daily feed so many who come
together to live like brothers?[5] Have we vast lands? rich
endowments? the benefices of churches? No. All we

have is this pure faith of his. It is we who receive the reward of his tears and fasts, we who gather each day the fruits of a prolonged poverty to which he held with such constancy. In order to show us that, wherever our vow of obedience may take us—even if the place affords us no temporal means of support—there can be no fear of want as long as we look to the Lord for what we need (as the proverb goes, 'whose bread we eat, his praise we carry on'). Let us be mindful then, that second in importance only to the mercy of the Lord is the steadfastness of Stephen, our shepherd's faith, and upon it we can rely, by Christ's grace, for our eternal salvation.

I pass over in silence the case of any of us trying to embark upon the road of freedom in his own wisdom, instead of our spiritual father's, which can offer such clear guidance and block all entry to the slavery of selfish desire. Even if such a person manages to set out, he certainly will not know how to finish the journey. This is why we witness so many who begin a life vowed to poverty, but do not persevere. We ought then, to be more pleased than we sometimes are to venerate the memory of this, our protector. Why am I mentioning this? So that we, as committed and generous religious, will give ourselves to the reading of Stephen's teachings, of which the present introduction speaks, and for the obvious reason that one can hardly love what is completely unknown. As the apostle says, 'faith comes from hearing',[6] and this is especially so when the faith in question is expressed in those anecdotes we have heard from Stephen's disciples concerning him, for they knew him with a certainty that comes from what they saw and heard for themselves. And in the conduct of those among them who are alive today we have evidence for the truth of what has been said. Though it may be true, too, that many of their tales can be applied only to one who possesses the perfected virtue of a 'man of God', and so cannot be imitated by everyone, even so, it is well within our power to admire what such tales speak of! Nor should we listen to them with indifference, but rather hold them dear, since they serve to give us a keener appreciation of our own frailty and, by the example of such a father, sharpen our insight into our own motives. The greater our progress toward God, the more we will mark our own shabbiness when confronted with another's goodness.

Take the case of the human body, in the close-knit unity of its parts: the hands and the feet, in spite of being themselves deprived of sight, still love the eyes that direct them to whatever they need.' So too with us: we love the surpassing worth of the venerable Stephen, since the grace that heaven bestowed upon him is of use to us all. Whoever disdains even to listen to a true saying will find it difficult, if not impossible, to put it into practice. This is said for the benefit of any who would waste time in such folly, though—God be thanked—arrogance like that would be hard to find among our brothers!

Hereafter, we will set out this work in chapters, largely composed of series of maxims, to make it easier for the reader to follow the progression of thought. Let us proceed, then, without further ado.

HERE BEGINS THE SPIRITUAL TEACHING OF STEPHEN, FIRST
FATHER OF THE GRANDMONTINE WAY OF LIFE. WITH ALL THE
STRENGTH OF NATURE AND GRACE GIVEN HIM BY GOD, HE STROVE
BY DEEDS, NO LESS THAN BY WORDS, TO LIVE OUT THE GOSPEL OF
CHRIST.

THERE IS NO OTHER RULE
BUT THE GOSPEL OF CHRIST

Brothers, I know that after my death there will be those
who will question you about which Order you belong to,
what Rule you adhere to. Some of these will do so out of
sincere interest, others simply to find fault. You should
humbly reply to either: 'You ask "which Rule?" as if there
were more than one, but there *is* no other besides the Rule
all Christians share. The Lord Jesus Christ is the unique
Way[8] upwards to the Kingdom of Heaven; he is the Gate[9]
through which each of us enters the Church. From no
other teacher, but him alone, have come that grace and
truth[10] which constitute the common Rule of all.' It may
happen, though, that someone persists, remarking that
we have it from blessed Gregory that Saint Benedict wrote
a Rule for monks. That is true, but that Rule can only be
called a rule at all because it derives from the Gospel.

All Christians who come together to live as one can be
called 'monks', even if the name is more particularly given
to those who, like the apostles, kept a greater distance from
the business of the world, giving their minds to the thought
of God alone.[11]

The first occasion we encounter in the Gospel where Jesus is preaching to his disciples, is in a sermon delivered on the institution of the monastic life: 'Blessed are the poor in spirit'[12] is the way, we might say, he began his Rule.

Had it been up to men to originate Rules, we would now have them in innumerable varieties, since in every age teachers have been free to teach howsoever they wish on the subject of spiritual progress, whether in discourse or the written word. If all of this teaching were considered normative, then it could be said, 'There are as many Rules as there have been prophets, apostles, and teachers'. If what Saint Benedict has produced is indeed a Rule, surely that term could be even more properly applied to what has come down to us from the Blessed Paul and John the Evangelist, both of whom spoke about the Lord in more complete and comprehensive ways.

Anyone, married or unmarried, can be saved by keeping the Rule of God, which is by no means the case with Benedict's Rule which, though certainly of great perfection, is plainly surpassed by the Rule of Saint Basil. Nevertheless all such Rules are derived from the Common Rule, the Gospel. Besides, only one Man is going to be saved, and that is Christ Jesus, together with his members, which leads us to understand that there can be only one Rule: that of the Son of God, who said, 'Without me you can do nothing'.[13]

Anyone who forsakes the instruction of God is judged to be outside the Rule, and whoever fulfills his commandments remains securely within it.

Chapter One

What needs to be said and pointed out to a novice newly-come to the Order

[1]   Jesus Christ affirms in the Gospel, 'Let whoever wants to come after me take up their cross and follow me'.[14] Our own shepherd, Stephen, spoke in a similar fashion to those whom he received into his novitiate. Whatever the petitioner's stated motive for appealing to Stephen's charity, before granting him admittance he would reply . . .

'Brother, how are you going to be able to bear this burden you wish to put upon yourself? Look at the Cross; it is often hard to remain upon it. If you come here, you will be nailed upon it, losing all of your autonomy, even the use of your eyes, mouth, and limbs. You will have to give up your own wishes regarding eating, fasting, sleeping, keeping vigil, and a multitude of other matters; not only that, but that which you valued in your worldly existence will disgust you henceforth. Next, you will never return to your family home and, should they come to you, you may not make them aware in any way of your present needs.'

[2]   'Brother, can you become a rustic, fetching wood and carting manure, a servant of all your brethren? All of this might come easily to you, but still,

you will remain in this prison without so much as a window through which to escape back to the world, unless you make it for yourself. Know, too, that I will not concern myself with you, nor will you allow yourself to be so with me, since you can see that I have torn my feet from the way of the world, and if I will not return there for my own sake, there is small chance that I would return for yours! And there is more yet. It may happen that I send you to some forested field, and when you have labored on it with a crude wooden hoe to make it yield, I may seize your harvest and give it to those who have spent the season here, taking care of me.'

[3]   'There remains something else even more dreadful, and it is a hundred times better for you to be condemned to live in the world than that this should befall you: He who falls from a greater height suffers greater injury. If you fall into Hell from here, you will be worse off than any who have been lost before you.

You can move on to any monastery you wish, where you will find impressive buildings, delicate foods served up according to their seasons. There too, you will meet with great expanses of land covered with flocks. Here you will find only poverty and the Cross.'

[4]   With words such as these, the Bonhomme[15] found out for himself if an aspirant had a firm intention to forsake the world. If anyone entered religious life because of some promise of earthly goods, Stephen would have considered him a simoniac. But if, after the aspirant arrives, he answers the customary ritual question regarding his

motives in such words as these: 'I desire to come here in order to endure all things; not so that I might increase,[16] but rather become smaller'. Then our shepherd received him as one of the brethren, and then instructed them as a group with words like these . . .

Chapter two

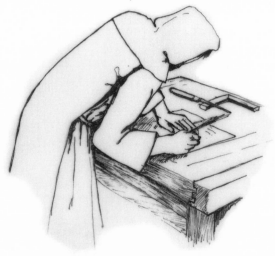

[1]   Religious life is grace, justice, and security. And when God draws anyone to it, he has brought such a one back to Paradise. Just as the Lord denied Adam whatever was unnecessary, so God treats those who desire to stand firm in truth in a like manner. As long as they are content with essentials they will remain in repose, but let them reach out for other, unprofitable things, and they are sure to fall into trouble and distress just as Adam did.[17]

Whoever delights in God[18] finds Paradise everywhere and lives the life of Heaven,[19] while the one who stands aloof from God finds Hell at every turning.

As a religious, then, you should be ever mindful that God is present and looking intently upon you as you work and speak; so too is an angel there, and a demon who craves to drag you from Paradise. For a demon never runs away from the good (even though it is so wholly estranged from the good) since this is precisely what it wishes to destroy.

[2]   How alert and careful you must become, under such thoroughgoing scrutiny! The former worldly ways of doing things will not suffice; new ways of talking, walking, sitting, seeing, working, praying—everything, really— have to be learned.

In the case of your conversation, a sturdy levee of reserve must be built to contain the flow of speech, so that what is said may always accord with truth.

No matter that it is a religious speaking words of advice or counsel, if these bear no fruit for speaker or hearer, in body or soul, they are worldly words nonetheless.

A religious, then, can be expected to move about with dignity and calm, and to work without fuss or commotion.

Should some object of desire come into view, the eyes must be shut up in a prison, by averting the gaze and fixing the attention upon something else.

When asking some favor of the Lord, there should be no audible disturbance made, since after all, it is the voice of the heart that God hears.[20]

What pleases God most about any prayer is the love it displays. Thus one who prays seeking another's harm does thereby shut out God altogether.

14

[3]   Everyone needs to take great care in these matters—
and others beside—lest any scandal is given in the community through bad example.²¹

If you enter the religious life and then refuse to change
in outward bearing, you are not likely to be transformed
in your inner attitudes either. In your mind at least, you
are still choosing the empty values of your age.

There are times when outward manner makes clear the
inner disposition. How can one be worldly in word and
deed yet be religious in thought? The body is easier to control at will than is the mind.

Chapter Three

The first test of novices

Once you have begun living in the monastery, the first trap a demon lays in your way is designed to rob you of the conviction you had even before leaving home, that religious life holds much that is good. When you, the novice, are confronted with the sight of the community working hard for the necessities of life, then the demon can work its will. For nothing is more trying for a newcomer than a thing which, though good in itself seems unpleasant in the doing.

No one wins a war who, in the first attack, falls and loses his weapons. You are a weakling indeed if you are sent sprawling by a sickly creature like a demon.

Chapter Four

A religious life will mean
confrontation with Evil

Here is a commendable meditation on religious life . . .

Think of a contest between two boxers for possession of a mountain. The match begins on the mountain top, and carries on, moving down through the hills, where sometimes one boxer, then the other, gains the upper hand. The outcome is uncertain until they reach the plain, and then it becomes clear which of them has won. Now, the mountain is the love of God, for whose sake one renounces the world. God draws you up this mountain in order to defend it against a demon, in hand-to-hand combat, just as a boxer defends his title. But you cannot remain at the summit when the demon is harassing you from all sides.

Yet as long as the downward running-fight is engaged (and this is what faith and deeds of kindness amount to) the human claim upon the love of God is being well defended. No wonder, though, that in the thick of conflict it seems that at times the demon has the advantage, while the human is sorely tried. But at length the Lord—for love's sake—will bring comfort and ensure your supremacy. And at the climax of the struggle—that is, at life's end—the demon will lie, wholly subdued, under foot.

CHAPTER FIVE

VARIOUS TRIALS THE NOVICE MUST ENDURE

When you are in love with the world, the enemy can freely seduce you. And should you quit your affairs, a demon, spurned, will set out in hot pursuit. Its name is 'Thousand Wiles' and it comes proffering diverse potions to find out which its victim will accept. When it knows which will offer most delight, it withdraws from the scene to return when you near your end, to lay you low at last.[22] Such is the creature's treachery, that it lets its victim remain quiet for so long in a good life. Much safer, then, when a demon fights hard from the start!

Chapter Six

How to avoid the snares of the Evil One

When the Evil One would set a trap, it is always set just outside the boundaries of something good. For instance, wishing to wear down its victim, it might suggest some pious practice that, though seemingly useful, will in no way suit him. There is good reason, then, for saying that to avoid such snares a great subtlety of mind is needed.

God exists in every place, even in the wicked, though not as if keeping company with him, since the two have nothing whatsoever in common. It is as the Gospel tells us: 'The light shone in the darkness, but the darkness knew it not'.[23] And while it is so, that a sinner who has spurned God's gracious help will compound his suffering thereby (becoming blind to that clear inner light that shines out in all directions for those of patient gaze), it is equally so, that with every good deed, the inner light's radiance grows, pushing back the dark invasion of Evil.

[2]   Nothing, not even honey in the comb, is sweeter than first advances of a demon. For if, at the start, its approach were to smite like a sword, its victim would be alerted by the pain and flee without carrying through on any of the demon's promptings.

A demon is so shrewd that it even prefers to do good to certain persons, if that will put them in the way of a single crime, so to possess them in the end. And should they come to their senses later, the demon tells them, 'You will by no means be condemned for this, when you have done these and these good works throughout your life'. If that fails, it rejoins, 'If you have any doubt on this score, you can always confess the deed before you die'.

[3]   Small chance that any demon would risk being recognized by saying to a genuine religious, 'Now, there is a fault for you to commit'. No, the way a demon starts its counseling is quite different. 'If you took up', it will say, '*that* way of life over there, think of what you could accomplish. You could keep longer vigils and fasts, and hold forth on the subject of God more than you ever could in this poor man's community, where you work without let-up, in the worst conditions day in and day out like common laborers, with a strict Rule to boot!' A speech like this is often enough to make us despise or even hate the good for which we came into religion.

[4]   A demon knows most certainly that there are those it will never win over, but it pesters them anyway, if only to hold them back from Divine Love. Consider how hard a demon will work to hinder someone from ascending to that heaven from which it has itself fallen. So, anyone who hopes to be saved should strongly resist evil, if for no other reason than simply to harass it, like a soldier who engages in tactics that have no other usefulness except to provoke the enemy.

Any of you who love God should do so knowing you will have no other recompense than the love itself.

[5]   To a demon offering counsel of any kind, you should respond as follows . . .

'O my enemy, well do I know that you are a fool. Why speak with me? Can you be ignorant of my present state? I have given myself; I am not my own. If it is a fight you want, go take it up with my superior, for I am his, and he will answer you. As for me, I am protected by his shield, and the word of God he speaks to me will shelter me from all your missiles.[24] The fiercer you come at me with your evil thoughts, the more disgraced and defeated your retreat will be.'

[6] A demon can be so sly that it will even induce some to enter community, just to haul them back out into the world again. Or, so that everyone might have the maximum misery, it keeps its ungovernable victims shut up with the brethren in the monastery. The loveless individual becomes more estranged from God when he lives among the upright—instead of with others like himself—and is yet unwilling to mend his ways. Judas, who lived with Jesus Christ, was just such a case.

If a person could become good, not by doing any good things, but merely by moving from castle to forest, this would imply that God has no greater insight into such persons than any of us have. Only let the demon lead the one it thinks it possesses into our house. At length the Lord will have converted the man, by gifting him with the grace of humility and with this he can trample all the fiend's snares, though they are more dense about him than are spiders' webs in summer.

Chapter Seven

Further snares to be avoided

There is another demon's snare which can be hard to recognize, and even harder to avoid. When someone leaves the world and has seriously begun a monastic life, there will come a time when his old acquaintances visit him at his new abode. Then the demon, playing the good mentor, says, 'This ought to make you happy, for a great benefit has come to this Order on account of you. No one from your country has ever come here before you arrived. Indeed, this is the last place your father and mother would have visited, had you not been here.' Those who have no experience of diabolical snares find considerable pleasure hearing themselves spoken of in this way, and then—crediting it as truth—fall into vainglory. This happens not only to one whose relatives come to visit, but they also befall those who have contact with seculars and form the opinion that a boon has come to the Order through them.

Chapter Eight

ABOUT THE SELF-CONCEIT THAT CAN ROB US OF OUR FAITH IN
GOD, IN OTHERS, AND EVEN IN OURSELVES

[1] Baseless self-conceit robs us of the trust that we owe
to ourselves, our companions, and to our Lord. Trust like
this is possible only when you can recognize and acknowledge that, of all the members of your community, you are
the foremost sinner.[25]

Surely if you are worthy of the name 'Bonhomme', you
will be more apt to spot your own faults than those of others,
and to consider any thief or whore to be your better.

But even so, you must never have such a low opinion of
yourself as to think that the loving hand of God cannot yet
reach out to help you. This mistake is often made by those
who despise sinners who can rise and go on trying after a
fall. The truth is, though, that it is the former, not the
latter persons, who have departed from God.

[2] It is no great accomplishment, is it, to be submissive
in a community of good people? In such a situation, trust
is only fitting. And even on the score of submissiveness,
you do well to reckon with admiration that it is *they* who
possess this virtue in an abundance and at a depth far ex-
ceeding your own.

This is the kind of behavior that can be expected from

those who have lived long and well in a community. The more concerned we have been to be always at the disposal of the Divine Guest in the house,[26] the easier it becomes to notice and acknowledge the contributions made by others toward that same goal. We see that each person has a place in the scheme of things, and a unique work to accomplish. Everyone except, perhaps, oneself—who provides little more than obstacles to the progress of others—but then, God can make use of anything to care for those he loves.

[3]   Conceit deprives your common life of all good faith and trust, but that is not all. It also makes faith in God impossible, since you deny thereby the credit God deserves for the good that can only have been done with divine help, and believe instead that you alone were responsible for it. Doubtless, there is not anyone who does not crave the praise of others, or some show of gratitude for whatever one secretly thinks 'only happened because of me'. But this, of course, is just vainglory, when you regard yourself as having qualities such as insight, influence, or good judgement, together with quantities of other gifts in suitably high degrees, when you do not. And you are even more gravely deceived when *others* believe such things about you.

The fact is that it is God who causes people to esteem you, for their own sake, to make it easier for them to believe what you say. Anyone, though, who has been the object of such trust will perish[27] if found to be unworthy of it.

[4]   It is by just such attractions and timely interventions

that God assists those who are his own. But, lest any of you topple into a devilish trap in the process, be advised: watch your conduct closely, and if others' admiration causes it to decline in goodness, be certain that you will earn only the painful reward of your neglect.

Believe this, too: if ever you come by some good in your religious life, it has been for the furthering of someone else's service of God. If, however, adversity has come your way, you have no one to blame but yourself.

[5]   No eloquence or written style can bring anyone nearer to God, but the recognition of personal sin, that prompts you to pray for God's help, will.

God is never more receptive to those who love him[28] than when they approve of nothing about themselves except those qualities that God has produced within them. These same persons wish neither that any good would come to them except by God's help, nor any salvation but from God's grace.

The Son of God who descended from Heaven, and knew how he would ascend there,[29] preached and taught that no one would ascend to Heaven unless he first humbled himself.[30]

And yet, however great anyone's humility might be, in God's sight, it is still pride. So we should reflect that no one is so wretched that could not be worse off. One look at the humility of Jesus Christ will show up our own as nothing. If you are as humble as you can be, however, God will dwell in you and allow you to share in the divine humility itself.

Chapter Nine

Another Conference for Novices

[1]   There are many who would rather teach and be damned than learn and be saved, wanting to be shepherds because they do not know how to be sheep, which is the first thing they needed to learn. Just so are those who enter religious life, right away wanting to lead before having learned to follow. Whenever I have someone like this standing before me, I say: 'You have lately come from the world, how can you teach what you do not yet know? Have you not abandoned the world's Rule—which you could ably teach us, should we ask—and come here, uninvited, to take up ours? Now take your lead from those who have gone before you—they know the way which you have yet to travel—and be happy if you can simply follow them. Stray to the right or the left, and you will find briars, thorns, and thieves awaiting to ambush you.'[31]

[2]   Keep in mind, too, how you behaved and made your own decisions when you were independent. But then, precisely because you were ignorant, you searched for a guide, whom you ought now to follow. For if you, the blind one, should stride out into the lead, you will fall into a pit,[32] and others will tumble in after you.

And are you not aware that there is no living creature

that prospers under its own governance?

The Good Angel became the Devil when he insisted on ruling himself, and Adam followed his lead, right out of Paradise.

[3] In fact, an indispensable counsel of the first order is never to take your own advice. In other words, if you want to follow the Lord Jesus Christ, have enough sense to let go of your own 'good sense', since you will only find yourself when you have thrown yourself away.[33]

If it is the Son of God you wish to imitate—he who emptied himself[34]—you will have to reduce yourself to nothing.

The greatest of goods necessary to us is the knowledge that we possess nothing good that God has not put within us[35] and maintained.

This is the main road God takes to come to us: our recognition of our own ignorance.

[4] Perhaps you are a novice who has felt repelled by something said or done in your monastery, contrasting it with the riches or power, the property or liberal education you had at your disposal in the world. Bear in mind though that with the help of any of these you would have had greater power to do evil, and a fuller potential for straying away from God! If you can find it in your heart to do so, repent of ever even possessing the wherewithal to contend with him.

Who would consider himself better off for having greater possibilities for the doing of evil than a pauper has?

There is nothing that can enrich or empower you more

surely than the love that binds you to God.[36] Let that bond be broken, and whatever else you may possess will bring you nothing but dishonor.

[5]　When we first become part of a community, Christ's Body,[37] it is not surprising that the animal in us[38] wants to control that Body. Even the first disciples would have gladly instructed the Lord—had he trusted himself to them[39]—and would have counseled him on how to avoid suffering and death.[40] The sort of advice they would have proffered to Jesus is exactly like the worldly wisdom many will give out regarding the demands of a religious life.

The disciples could not understand the works of God, even when they saw them displayed, until after they had gone through that state of distress over Jesus' death, and then received the Holy Spirit. So, too, for us, who have long been charmed by sin; it is beyond our capacity to understand the sweetness of God[41] until we have gone through the distress caused by taking our share in the cross of Jesus.[42] This is why the Lord did not gift the apostles with the Holy Spirit while he was still with them, but waited until they came to an acceptance of his death, their own grief, and his final bodily departure from them.

[6]　Waterlogged kindling recently brought indoors will not flame up until the heat has dried it out. Likewise ourselves, soaked through with sinfulness, we are unable to glow with God's love until his warmth has dried us out again.

No one can see anything with eyes shut, but the open

eyes see nothing if their object is not lit up. It is when the light reflected by the object joins with the eyes' light,[43] that vision occurs. Apply the same principle to spiritual vision; as long as you possess this faculty in some small degree, it will enable you to perceive deeper meanings in what you hear. In contrast, a worldly person may be told, regarding some trifling matter, 'Friend, that is not permitted', but the meaning of these words remains obscure, since the inner light of perception has been extinguished by many other, darker thoughts.

[7]   It can happen that a newcomer, behaving as though still in the world, defends his worldly values. However, someone who has persevered long in keeping the Rule challenges the novice by offering a coherent defense of monastic observance, demonstrating it by words and deeds, helping the person to grow used to hard work of body and spirit.

Unless a novice is hopelessly perverse, kindliness is more likely to elicit his trust than any other approach. If it takes a benefactor some doing to win the trust of a sceptic, what success would a bully have?

This is the worst kind of arrogance: to receive correction and then refuse to improve, not because you have forgotten your training, but because pride has erased even the memory of it.

Humility always fears abandoning its principles; pride could not care less, whatever anyone says.

Chapter Ten

[1]   True as it is that the more we love God, the wiser and more devout we become, still, to no other endeavor is a prior training so needful as to a life dedicated to serving God.

The Lord entrusts all who have faith with spiritual goods and gear, fitting them to abide in his love, in the same way that a rich man decorates his castle with suitable furnishings.

We religious are negligent in nothing so much as this: we understand very little about those things with which God has endowed us, so that we might be able to render him a thorough-going service. Ignorant about what God has really given us, we begin to work with some implement that never came from him. It is not long after this that we shyly abandon it, exhausted and abashed. What has happened is that we have mistakenly taken some virtue for granted, while neglecting another that God wishes us to use.

[2]   The Lord never apportions the full complement of virtues to any one person, for if it were possible to take up virtues at will, pride would certainly destroy him.

God is like a mother who refuses to allow her child to handle even a small knife, for the little one could cut himself with it. So when you are denied something you have prayed for, consider yourself well-served by a compassionate God who knows the harm it would do you.

One of us receives one sort of strength from God, someone else receives another. The whole Jesus Christ consists, after all, in the sum of all the community members together.[44]

[3]   God wants us to rejoice more in the good we hold in common with others in faith and unity, than in any personal virtue we may possess independently of them.

Virtue possessed in isolation serves no useful purpose, just as an eye is useless for seeing if it is taken out of the head.

The eyes are just as pleased by the ears' hearing as by their own power of vision and, because of their union, the eye walks, the foot sees, bones hear, ears speak, and if something is lacking to one member all the others come to its aid. But let any of the members abandon its particular duty, and none of this solidarity is possible.

If you have been charged with the duty of being the hands or feet or any other member of the Body of Jesus Christ, and then quit your place, the Lord and all your fellow members will blame you for his dismemberment, for you have, in effect, forsaken him and, as far as you could, also dishonored the Body.[45] Now, the Lord is quite wise enough to choose someone else to take your place; you, however, will never have that privilege again, for by the time you reconsider, the Body of Jesus will have moved on, to a greater degree of glory.[46]

[4]   Each of you has to test your own virtues and so learn how it will be best to journey to God.

Any traveler coming upon a bog, first probes its depth, to learn if it is indeed impassable, aware that the whole company will be delayed if one of them falls into the mire. We religious need to be like that, putting our own gifts of nature and grace to the test, so to use them without hindering each other.

You cannot diminish the share of virtue that by right belongs to some other member of the community without damaging what you have in common.

The body owes it to the soul to keep vigil, to fast, and to work.

God is determined to hold you fast in the upright life wherein everyone needs to practice the corporal works of mercy. That being so, it is hardly likely that God will not expect the same constancy from you, according to your abilities.

There are those who would embark upon a contemplative life before making progress in their active lives. Let them look within, though, and they will recognize neither Martha nor Mary.

The more exemptions you have from doing any work, the more nasty thoughts you are bound to accumulate.

If you have never learned how to look after 'junior's' (that is the body's) comportment, you will handle 'senior's' (the soul's) with great difficulty.

[5]   For the sake of your religious commitment, look to your own welfare in matters of food, sleep, and clothing,

finding out how much you need to support your resolve to persevere. For our God is faithful,[47] not cruel, and he wants us to serve him joyfully—not only with awe[48]—without complaint from body or soul.

Anyone who cannot bear up under the service of God when the necessities of life are provided will hardly hold up for long if all of that is lacking.

It is better for you to have enough to eat, and with it be obedient, than to fast overmuch while being critical of others and inattentive at worship.

Ascetic abstinence has nothing to do with going beyond some minimum limit. In short, to be concerned with measuring one's spiritual accomplishments brings blame upon those deeds.

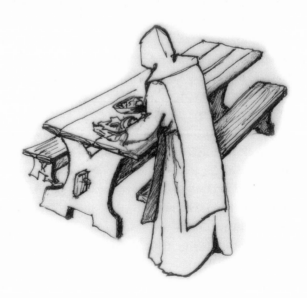

Chapter Eleven

A conference on mutual correction

[1] Suppose you correct a brother, as lovingly as you can, and he gets angry. Assume that it was your manner of correcting that set off such a temper, and blame yourself for it. Clearly, your reproof was not as measured and gentle as it should have been if you wanted it to have a gracious hearing. Admit this, then and there, and it might be interpreted as humble regret, allowing God—if he sees good will come out of it—to calm the situation. On the other hand, if you go on and excuse yourself for this provocation, should you one day find yourself angered by some reproof addressed to *you*, make sure that you credit your own sin for whatever vexation you feel.

[2] Truth is always a sweet thing. If you find it hard to take, it is only because inside you are feeling shame for your failings. You are like a sick person who, because of the bile in your system, finds food bitter that is sweet to someone who is healthy.

To the unseeing eye, nothing is clear.

There are religious who cannot take in the proper teaching about our way of life, fearing that once they know it they will be bound to live by it. Such persons are, in effect, imposters.

It is not likely that you will do something that you cannot even bear hearing about!

[3]   It is plain stupidity, wanting to listen to a sermon
railing against faults you never commit, rather than to
one touching on your own misdeeds, when a sharp lecture
about those would do you more good. You are in the best
position to profit from a rebuke if you have rebuked yourself for the same deed before time.

[4]   If you do not want to be corrected by anyone, you
would do well to become the sort of disciple whose life is
above reproach.
    Discipline is not meant to shame us, but to rid us of
shame.
    If you poke a stick into a water filter and cloud the wa-
ter, it is not because you have put ash in, but because you
have stirred up what was there already. So it is when you
are annoyed by some reproach; the vice your friend has hit
upon still lies within you, not wholly purged.

[5]   No one should hanker after the praise of another, any
more than one would criticism. You would be
rightly called a fool if you deliberately acted
in a manner certain to earn censure; you
are just as much of a simpleton if you
do good in order to be praised.
    People who bristle when they are
blamed will be agreeable just as long
as they are praised.

Chapter Twelve

About the tenderheartedness God shows to those who choose religious life

[1] On top of all the other mercies each of us has received, God gives something more to us who have chosen the religious life. Once we have embraced the vocation, everything about monastic custom and worship that formerly seemed dreadful and intolerable now becomes appealing; what used to frighten us not at all, now gives us no end of trouble. You will not really be able to believe this just by being told it is so; you need to experience it. You can at least consider the following example. The women who went to the tomb of Jesus, wishing to anoint the body,[49] were more anxious about how they would move away the boulder than about anything else, and this was the very thing that was resolved for them first. Whereas of the body of Jesus that they were so sure would be there, they found no trace. Think, too, of those disciples who fled when the Lord told them that unless they would eat of his flesh and drink his blood they could not have eternal life.[50] If they did flee, they had to return later, since God has no greater way by which to express his tenderheartedness toward them.

[2] At the beginning, truth is hard for us to take; after a while, though, it recovers its eternal sweetness. Untruth

and misconduct, on the other hand, are pleasant at first, but then later they are a constant anxiety to us.

If you are finding your monastic training difficult, just think back to how hard you had to work when you were in the world, and compare that with how slight your burdens are now. Think, too, that Jesus went through even the Passion without sin.[51]

It is nothing extraordinary when we put up with the misery we have deserved,[52] or that by our sins we deserve it every day.

Those who persevere in monastic life can say in their heart about the trouble they have had in doing so: 'Blessings on you, God, for keeping me from pursuing the delights that might land me in Hell'.

Chapter Thirteen

Comparing a genuine religious to a raw army recruit

[1]   An inexperienced soldier has no fear of leaving a place of safety and, without any order, rushing out into the midst of the enemy, only to be set upon and captured by them. As a religious, you are secure while you remain in the monastic enclosure, if doing so is a free choice; if it is not, this imperfect motive will be the breach through which a demon will launch its siege.

In fact, unless you have chosen it for yourself, enclosure is nothing but a prison.

[2]   Say you hear tell that an old friend back home is warring with the worst of your own former enemies, and you contrive to back your friend's cause, wishing for your enemy's harm. In so doing, you become an even worse enemy to that friend of yours, not only because such behavior does spiritual damage, but when you drive your monastic values from your heart like that, you make war on those who remain in the world, just as though you were pelting them with stones and spears. So, because these things can happen, for your own good, avoid hearing the latest gossip from home.

You may fall into a demon's clutches through a single stray thought; return to the world physically as well, and you will be that demon's prisoner for good.

Chapter Fourteen

God is faithful to each one of us

[1]   God keeps faith with each one of us. He never counsels me to damn myself in order to save someone else. Far from it, my first responsibility is to see to my own salvation by loving the Lord above all else and doing good to others.[53] Only then may I stretch out my hand to my neighbor, and draw him along with me into the Kingdom of Heaven.

When God commands you to love your neighbor as yourself[54] this is not too much to ask, for you are enjoined to love only what is good in others.

A good deed belongs as much to the one who loves it as to the doer of that deed, so why not cherish every bit of goodness as your property? This is why a Bonhomme, hearing of another's good deed, will praise the Lord in his heart, saying: 'Blessed be you, my God, for this good is mine, too, and he who, for love of you, did the work, did so for both of us'.

[2]   If you are living properly, it behooves you to thank God not only when you hear tell of a good person, but even when you hear of a bad one. Rejoice over goodness because it is yours, too; accept the bad as well, for in this way you protect yourself from it (and from worse besides).

After all, no one has murdered or stolen anything from you, nor have you yourself harmed anyone else.

[3]   In truth, it is quite impossible to steal anything from good people. If they are heir to family estates, they by no means reckon these as personal wealth. No one can plunder them of their spiritual riches either; indeed, as in the case of Job, should their temporal fortunes diminish, their spiritual treasure grows apace. How much more will this be so, then, for those who would be poor and downtrodden for the Lord's sake? He will enrich them with even greater spiritual good, so that they can patiently bear their material poverty.

Chapter Fifteen

God cherishes the whole human race

We can get some idea of the love God
bears us, when we consider that whatever any of us does for another's true
welfare, be it material or spiritual,
God considers our deed a personal favor.[55] When, on the
other hand, we do what is
harmful to ourselves, God is
vexed, since we do not live for
ourselves alone.[56] And he is
even angrier if ever we turn away from him[57] for the sake
of empty idols.[58]

God shows us so much genuine affection and works so
hard on our behalf; this ought, above all, to shame us in our
sins. For God contrives so much good for us, and speaks to us
of his tender feelings,[59] only to receive so much evil in return.

If our life seems good so,
God alone has made it so,
For we are the ones he loves so,
and God loves
putting love's gifts
into loving hands.

Chapter Sixteen

About the 'hundredfold' in the Gospel

It is natural for us to want to have the goods of this world, both for enjoyment and for physical survival. Further, everyone takes a special joy in children, or spouse, or some other good. But to us who have renounced these goods to follow him, God adds to the joy we would have had, immeasurable joy beside. Whenever trials come, he gives us the victory, or shields us from any who would lay us low, and so we enjoy our success and are secure in the salvation promised by the Lord to his faithful followers. Such, then, is the 'hundredfold' mentioned by Jesus in the Gospel.[60]

Good folk take more pleasure in the salvation they hope to have, but have not yet got,[61] than the wicked could ever take in their worldly possessions, even if they had all there was[62] to own.

Chapter Seventeen

How fearsome, to be separated from God!

Estrangement from God is such a dreadful notion, it would be unimaginable, were it not for the daily evidence of sight and hearing, that some do indeed make so bold as to stand aloof from him.

In his gracious goodness God willingly partook in the human lot of poverty[63] and affliction; but we are so proud, so haughty, that we want nothing to do with the riches[64] and glory of a God like that!

Chapter Eighteen

Why we can trust in the Lord

God is going to enable us to reign with him[65] in Heaven forever. Now, there is one reason above all others why we can believe this: because the Lord humbled himself[66] so completely as to dwell in us, who are only clay pots, and to dwell in this world.[67]

CHAPTER NINETEEN

ABOUT OUR LOVE FOR GOD

If it is God we wish to love with all our heart, then we cannot love anything else, for if we love many things (no matter what) there is no way we are ever going to give them up[68] for God's sake, and then want nothing more besides him. But a love of things could never fulfill our heart's desire, since it is always open to further seduction. Only love for God fills us totally and expels all greed from our souls.

Chapter Twenty

How sweet are God's commandments

[1]   The amazing thing, you must admit, is that God's commandments are so pleasant and easy to keep. What if God had said, 'Unless there is a crowd around you listening as you pray, I will not even give you a hearing; nor will I acknowledge your almsgiving, if there is not a large audience present watching you pay them out'. It would be hard indeed, to be forever having to gather a crowd together every time you wanted to do a good deed. But as things are, God has prescribed anonymity to all who would do good.[69] If he had said, 'I will not accept a good deed unless everyone is watching you do it', we would have had a much harder time of it.

[2]   Likewise, it is easier to be poor and lowly than to be rich and proud. Consider their respective requirements. Humility demands that you reject the living you could have inherited. Pride, however, must amass a surfeit of goods; this is hard to accomplish. Humility bids the wedding guest take a lesser place at the banquet table;[70] pride demands to be moved up higher, which takes more trouble to effect. You have Jesus to thank and praise for this state of affairs, for he certainly never said, 'The more well-heeled, well-spoken, or well-born you are, the greater you will be

in the Kingdom of Heaven'. No, since it is easier for us to lose status than to gain it, he promised most to the least among us.[71]

Chapter twenty-one

Who is deserving of condemnation?

If, instead of learning repose from the Lord,[72] you prefer to let a demon goad you into agitation, then you will be condemned to it eternally.

Lying is harder work than telling the truth, since a lie must be very carefully concealed if it is not to be discovered, whereas truth is meant to remain out in the open and unembellished.

Jesus Christ's advice to us, to enter by the sheepfold gate,[73] is easier to follow than a demon's suggestion, that one can enter by throwing oneself down from a great height.[74]

Chapter twenty-two

Cast your cares upon the Lord[75]

From us who believe in him, the Lord demands an unfettered love. To that end we must load even our worldly cares upon him, letting him manage our affairs. By asking this he does us a much greater kindness than if he said, 'You may love me as soon as you have seen to your own needs'.

Chapter Twenty-three

How sweet God's Rule can be[76]

The best way to understand just how sweet the Lord really is,[77] is to note that there are some who find God's Rule so sweet that they are content with nothing else, not even the people and things they love most in this world such as spouses, books, and the rest. Considering how the love of God can make some persons oblivious to the doings of their loved ones, one could get the idea that the Elect in Heaven's realm might fail to feel sorry for Hell's inhabitants.

Chapter twenty-four

How to find the Lord

Provided you know how, it is much simpler to find the Lord within, where he is nearer, than it is to go abroad looking for him. But we can be so foolish, wanting to look for our happiness and repose in the void outside ourselves, rather than within, where they will be found. Nor are we keen to undertake what we most surely know will be a thankless task, that is, rejecting worldly ways. However, it is with such efforts that you will gain possession of the Lord, who is the joy beside which all other things seem disagreeable.

Chapter Twenty-Five

Patience and the works of Christ

[1]   It is good if you can find your enjoyment in the works Christ gives you to do.

He has sent his disciples out like lambs among wolves.[78] Now, if you or I were arranging a fight with wolves, there is no way we would pick lambs for such combat, if we wanted to win. But the Lord, thinking of the greater glory[79] it will bring, prefers to overcome wolves using lambs, not bears or lions.

[2]   Since lambs cannot carry heavy loads, God relieves them of any worldly worries that would be a burden to them. Their victory will be won solely by their willingness to persevere.[80]

Patience is so great a virtue that whoever lacks it cannot be self-possessed either. And if you lack yourself, what will you serve God with?

Chapter Twenty-six

The words of God contain such sweetness!

[1]   There is such sweetness in the divine word. Consoled by that sweetness we can accept that the Lord has placed no limit on the doing of good.

A criminal, dying unexpectedly, reproaches God for this. But the good praise him in their hearts, saying, 'O God, how great is your mercy, not wishing us to know anything about our death, rather keeping the eventuality before our minds, so that each of us might live more securely in the desire for your rest'.[81]

[2]   It is inconceivable that God would demand that we be ever-vigilant in our service of him, as if we knew when our end would come; after all, we often separate ourselves from him when we are ignorant of the hour and the day.[82]

Nothing pleases the honest person more than the fact that God has asked for a constant goodness. If God had said, 'Give yourself a day off from good works', he would have seemed to be saying, 'Abandon your happiness and settle down with an ill-temper instead'.

[3]   The cross of Jesus is the 'rest' he wants to give us.

The wicked say, 'If God will let us know the day we are to die, then we will turn to him'. But it is hardly believable that they would stick to that commitment. Even if they knew for certain they had a year of life remaining, they would still be unsure of what each day would bring, and would soon desert God.

Chapter Twenty-Seven

In God's Service there are no limits

Seeing that God is always so necessary to us, and always so willing and able to help, it is astounding that we do not always love him.

We are endlessly wanting salvation from God (even after a thousand years of enjoying his glory we would refuse to be banished)[83] so it would be unjust that God, for his part, should put any limit or remission upon the service he expects from us.

Chapter Twenty-Eight

How to tell the truth

If you would speak the truth, pray God that you tell it truly. For unless your actions uphold your words, you have spoken falsely. Take a line from a psalm: 'My eyes are always on the Lord'.[84] Now, however true God's words are, if you say them from a heart at odds with God, you speak falsely. A thing you call good is not good for you if in your heart it pleases you little.

Chapter Twenty-Nine

How to derive a good example from a bad one

Sometimes great wisdom consists in learning a good action from seeing an evil one. Consider the saying: 'He who plots some betrayal or sin takes great pains lest anyone learn of it and hinder him, even if that person could be of some use'. Now, if that is how someone guards a wicked deed, then surely, when you would do a good deed, you must take care not to show it off, in case vainglory snatch it from you.

CHAPTER THIRTY

HOW TO MAKE USE OF THE EXAMPLE OF YOUR SENIORS

[1]   Whoever you are, when you enter religious life, if you cannot find examples of goodness in the deeds of those around you, you can at least note their conspicuous wickedness and take your lesson from that, in this way. Be convinced that your carefulness and hard work must be as great as all the wrongdoings they have allowed to go on (to their loss) and persisted in for their own selfish purposes.

[2]   The 'Bonhomme' should always be talking either with God in prayer, or about God in conversation.

CHAPTER THIRTY-ONE

WHY WE ARE ALL BLIND TO OUR FAULTS

In the spiritual life, there is no better way to identify your greatest hindrance than this. It is the one thing you never notice. In fact, it is the frequency of a flaw that makes it undetectable. It is only when you have finished with a fault that you notice it. It is like living in darkness; until you have emerged from it, it is imperceptible.

Chapter thirty-two

How to listen to God's word

If you are well-intentioned, your first response to God's word will be to assess yourself according to its measure. Listen with a bad will and you are bound to twist the words around, to exonerate yourself while blaming someone else.

Chapter Thirty-three

The flaws to be found in good deeds

It is more perfect to find something to blame yourself for in a good deed than in a bad one. For anyone can feel guilty after committing evil, but it takes wisdom to recognize how much ill still lies beneath a good action.

In the good you do, have the humility to spy out your faults, and you will guard your virtues.

Chapter Thirty-Four

Attitudes that make God's guidance pleasant to follow

[1]   Think often about how pleasant and easy God makes things for you.

It is easier to take yourself apart and inspect your own inner dispositions than it is to examine someone else in this way, much simpler, and of more use to you, which is why God—whose demands are always light[85]—has commanded it. A demon, in contrast, will suggest that you give up on the plank in your own eye,[86] so as to be off clearing away someone else's.

Many of us are more inclined to go abroad and, in a flurry of activity, take charge of others, instead of staying home and peacefully settling down to self-improvement.

There are two different motives for correction: correcting another for charity's sake; and correcting another out of ill-will, envy, or vainglory, in which case the corrector's guilt is great.

[2] Whenever you catch yourself starting to complain about someone, you would do well to turn inward and inspect your own thoughts and deeds. And, when you have thoroughly done this, you will discover that the person you were grumbling about is far ahead of you in the race.[87]

[3] It is better to be defeated, but win in the end, than to triumph at first, but finally lose. Soldiers who must retreat at first, then later rally and vanquish their enemy receive more honor than those who flee the battle and are later hunted down and wiped out.

Chapter Thirty-Five

How to be on God's highway

[1]   Those who travel God's highway need to take care not to allow either boredom to slow them down, or over-confidence to trip them up.

When harvest time comes, no farmer expends all his energy cutting the first ear of grain. Nor did Saint Peter earn his reward all at once on the day he was crucified; day by day he collected the ears of grain, binding the sheaf only at his end.

[2]   The first stage on the road to God is a dread of having to pay the painful price of sin, whereby one has advanced far enough to be alarmed at the prospect of Hell, and so forsakes wrongdoing. This is a good start, but no one ought to settle for it. What would be better would be to advance to the love of God, and do the works of love for justice's sake. Martha did just that when she offered hospitality to Jesus Christ and lovingly attended to his needs.[88]

[3]   Pride can turn even our highest motives into a snare. So, our first priority has to be to forget all worldly anxiety, and delight in God alone. This is that 'perfect love'[89] that will, once we possess it, preserve us from any sort of a hell.

When you love God perfectly, it will seem to you that you possess no love whatsoever. The more ardently you are affected by spiritual desire, the more it will seem that you are lost and distanced from God.

[4]   It is the Lord's wish that in this life we should—far from ever being fully satisfied in our love—rather hunger and thirst always for justice.[90] Recall how your father would proffer you an apple or some other treat when you were a child and then, to increase your excitement, snatch it back just before you took it. God's purpose is something similar, when he withdraws from those who love him best, thus firing them up even more, meanwhile never failing to support and console them.

Chapter Thirty-Six

Almsgiving and the monastic life

[1]   Those who live the monastic way do so more perfectly when they support themselves by receiving alms,
instead of being in a position to give them.[91] And this is
why, while you were an independent person in the world,
able to do good or evil at will, you could give alms, make
long prayers and the like as you pleased. But once you
forsook the power to choose good deeds or bad for the
sake of something better—self-donation to the Lord—
you became unable to give alms, however much God es-
teems and welcomes such deeds.

[2]   Formerly, when you gave alms, regardless of the size
of the amount you offered, you always held something
back for yourself, or at least held on to yourself. But when
you let go even of this, and cast yourself at Jesus' feet in
order to listen to his words[92] and do his will, he will no
longer ask that you return to the worries of a Martha,[93]
that is, the good you could still do in the world.

Jesus Christ praised Mary more highly for sitting at his
feet and attending to his words[94] than he praised Martha
for all her ministrations, while she thought her sister did
nothing.[95] Further, Mary never feared that the Lord would
say, 'Get up and help her'. He said nothing of the kind; in

fact, he defended her saying that, though her sister did well, Mary was better off.

[3] When a Bonhomme, whom God has chosen for praise,[96] receives material goods sent to him from outside the monastery, he refuses to accept them and returns them to their giver. He never thinks to himself, 'so and so will get me what I need', but puts himself in the gracious care of God alone and makes his request to those who hold office in his house.

God takes care of good folk and does everything for their sakes. He even looks after the wicked who have parted ways with him (thereby losing control of their own bodies,[97] no less than of other matters), however much they may still be able to destroy themselves further.

Chapter Thirty-Seven

The poor of Christ

[1]   The poor of Christ, who have renounced themselves, giving the most generous alms they could, possessing nothing of their own—neither their own selves, nor any other thing—should be most happy that they can no longer give alms, unless someone else provides them with the wherewithal.

There are persons who risk losing God in order to be in a position to do, admittedly, good works (like speaking to others about God or lavishing alms upon them) but doing them out of self-importance.

There are others again who gain the Lord by the good they neither do, nor see how they might do. These are the poor of Christ, people who notice others' needs and want to help. But, because they are now powerless, God considers their good will as if this was the doing of the deed itself. Who knows? If they would have had the means to do good, they might have lost their goodness of heart!

Nothing produces good will like poverty of spirit.

[2]   If those who have been freed of material obligations go back to looking for ways to give alms, clearly their gift of self is weak. They may as well have kept the wherewithal to do such things. For had their renunciation been com-

plete, they would now have nothing—neither hand nor foot—with which to give.

Chapter Thirty-Eight

About the shepherd's attitude toward the community

The shepherd (who is at liberty to do so) may give to the poor outside the monastery, but must be always on guard not to harm those inside thereby. All the good that is done is done as by a communal act, and care must be taken in such cases that the community not be disadvantaged in the process. Certain members, when they observe that alms have been given, may be agreeable to it at the time, but later take offense when they discover they now lack something, and will complain: 'We are now poor ourselves on account of what our shepherd has given away'.

It comes naturally to a wise person, to be so careful in the doing of good that no one is harmed thereby.

Chapter Thirty-Nine

The reward of good example

Live an exemplary life and you will receive your reward from those who hear of it, from both the good and the bad alike. The good will follow you; the bad will refuse to follow, but of their own accord. On your side, God considers all of them saved by your example; on the side of those who chose not to accept the peace of your fidelity, that peace will return to you.[98]

Chapter Forty

Good advice for everyone

Nothing pleases God more than when someone willingly abandons serious sin, except perhaps when we overcome the sorts of temptations that are forever looming: to silly conversation, bad temper, or the like. For this latter is a renunciation of oneself.

Chapter Forty-One

The sufferings of Hell and Heaven's joys

If any of you who have earned a place in Hell should have a preview of its pains and torments, their intensity and duration, you would die on the spot, paralyzed with fear. But say you are among the saved, and are allowed a look at the happiness of Heaven, its intensity and endurance, then forthwith you would pass away from the sheer pleasure of it all. Bodily beings, you see, living this earthly existence, cannot bear too close a look at spiritual realities.

Chapter Forty-Two

The love of God is there for the taking

[1]   In the marketplace of this world, God pits his own love against the attractions of silver and gold and other earthly things; in this way he makes it dearer and more valuable to those who would possess it. For when they want to covet something, some earthly thing, God is there to confront them with a choice, as if to say, 'Choose now which you would prefer: me, your God, or the temporal thing. Should you choose me, I will give you more than you could ever covet; choose the other, and you will lose everything'.

[2]   God gives to each according to that person's needs, so you are not ever going to be condemned for making a lot of money, provided you harm neither yourself nor anyone else in the process. In fact, this is how God contrives to spend on many the wealth amassed by one. Whoever has made a fortune by cheating and exploiting others, unwittingly has wasted it; the one who gathers wealth, yet spends it, too, on doing good, will have God as a business partner.

[3]   You can desire the goods of this world and still be

truly poor in spirit. You need only desire to serve God with what you possess, having nowhere in your heart a wish to risk anyone's salvation or to evade God's commandments.

If ever you find yourself wanting to sin, instead of conjuring up thoughts of damnation or suchlike, you ought to think like this: 'I will not do this thing, for if I do, the love I bear within me for God will be diminished'. This is the sort of 'Fear of God' that will protect you!

If you are ashamed to sin, you will never bear the shame of sinning.

Chapter Forty-Three

God's gracious help and kindness
is unique to each of us

[1]   God relates to each of us uniquely, as if making a contract with you personally, which would read: 'You may use this benefit to work beside me as far as it enables you, and if you work as hard as you can, I—your God—will finish everything you cannot. My saving love will act on your behalf, but I will give you all the credit for the deed. If, however, you fail to make use of what I have given you, even if I were to give you more, it would only add to your downfall.'[99]

[2]   In all those cases wherein God entrusts more to one than to another, we need to examine the order underlying God's action. If you are already wealthy, consider whatever God puts in your hands[100] as meant for the needs of the poor. So put your hope in God and give to the poor with confidence. The poor, for their part, should believe that God permits their indigence to provide the rich with occasions to supply their needs.

All wealth, wherever it is found, belongs to God.

[3]   If you should change your state of life and donate your estate to the poor, all that will have mattered about your deed in God's sight will be the quality of your will.

For no one can make a heap of alms that will reach Heaven;[101] but good will, that gives alms solely for God's honor, will make its way through to the highest heaven.

You can be sure that the rich have more to gain from the poor, than the poor from them.

[4]   As with wealth, so too with strength for working, or wisdom for putting things into words; you can be certain that, if you possess endurance or discernment, others have earned it for you, and that God has given it as much for the sake of others as for your own. The same principle applies to any other virtue.

[5]   Each benefit that you enjoy will be useful only if you distance yourself from it, by believing that it was given you by God for the service of others. It may even be better for you to be convinced that, unless you can guard virtues from arrogance (which would prevent their profiting someone else), you could actually deserve condemnation for possessing them.

Take your share of the blame for any evil that touches your life—and genuinely believe that you deserve it—and as your reward God will free you from its effects.

Chapter Forty-Four

How to think about yourself

It is easier to see what you are than what you are failing to be.

Recognize yourself as a sinner and you will be acquainted with truth.

All human righteousness consists in believing that God alone is righteous.[102]

Chapter Forty-Five

The reward your almsgiving can earn

[1]   When you come to be laid in the earth, you can have no better friend than the one who left your house, only to return: that is, your almsgiving. The demons are never far off who would gladly carry your soul away. Only your almsgiving never really deserts you. In fact, it goes ahead, setting your soul behind it, shielding it against the demons who would burst upon you, driving them away, saying, 'Did you not see me here?' and then telling you, 'Do not be afraid'.

Finally arriving at your judgement, a demon will make its accusations, saying, 'In such and such ways this soul did me homage'. But your almsgiving will reply, 'Regardless of what she has done, I make her exempt from all that her sins deserve'.

[2]   You would do well to get yourself a comrade like this!

Often the miser who refuses to give what is, after all, his share only, is withholding bread and wine to Jesus Christ who, for his part, freely gave his flesh and blood for us.

There are some who would worry more about the seasoning and tastiness of their food than about their souls, and they die with hands full of wealth. When they awake from death, though, and have gone forth from this world, they will find nothing in their hands but emptiness.

CHAPTER FORTY-SIX

HOW THE FOOLISH DIFFER FROM THE WISE

The foolish and the wise may differ in many respects, but certainly in this; when something good is done, fools see their own action, not God's.

When fools want to give alms to persons who do not greatly need them and could bear the lack, God challenges them, saying: 'What are you doing with the fortune I entrusted to you? Where are you planning to take it? Help me to care for this pauper here, who is stricken with worse hunger, cold, and misery, and for whom I lack a visitor'. But the fool will respond: 'Am I to give my help where you wish it? Devil take the one who would act so; I would rather be off assisting where I alone will get the thanks for it.'

[2]   Alms given wilfully like this will not profit the giver at all. This will only be realized when he has thrown away what goods he had to give. Thereupon God will say: 'If you would have done my pleasure, I and all my angels would have praised you, but since you acted on your own ideas, you will not even have the reward you sought'.

And so it is that the fool builds on sand.[103] However little the praise he receives from anyone at all will be enough to topple his house of good deeds.

Chapter Forty-Seven

How the wise think things through

[1]   Be it about ever so small an act of generosity, if you are wise you will think it through. 'This I will give for the sake of my soul; though it be hardly anything at all, still I know God wants it, so I will do it if I can and at least keep myself from shriveling up inside.'

If you decide on giving a big sum, you must be more prudent still, careful not to waste your gift through a sloppy choice of a beneficiary. Say to God in your heart: 'God, where would you have me return this wealth to you? Or to which of your members is it more needful? for that is the one I want to spend it on.'

[2]   While you are sagely weighing up all the practicalities, your alms will sprout, flower, and bear fruit[104] in your hand.

The poor folk to whom you give may be feeling abased in their poverty, so it would be a great act of compassion if you in your turn could give with self-abasement, taking care not to be recognized.

God makes plain the good works that we hide,[105] and consigns to oblivion those we show off.

[3]   If you want to be worthy of respect, make the Lord your only aim, always searching for ways to advance his cause.

Chapter Forty-Eight

On helping the poor

[1]   Coming to the aid of the poor in preference to your own kin is the more excellent thing to do.

Holy Writ by no means forbids us to help those who are close to us—indeed, it takes this for granted—but even so, it is considerations of the flesh that draw us to this sort of loving, in which the left hand grabs what is the right's, so to speak; and this, Jesus Christ forbids.[106]

[2]   It is good to come to the aid of any who ask your help—orphans and widows, and other poor folk—with even more than just the bare necessities. It is even better, though, and more welcomed by God, to put one's gifts of nature and grace at the service of the One who saves our souls.

Chapter Forty-Nine

GOOD SENSE IS NEEDED TO CARRY A GOOD WORK THROUGH[107]
FROM START TO FINISH

[1]   When you set about doing something good, you will need more than a little determination, and great steadfastness while you are seeing it through; else you may give up on the way.

[2]   In this matter of foresight, say you want to go to Jerusalem or another holy site for prayer. First you should think about all the time you will have to spend attending church services, the money you will spend in offerings, and the various other matters you will have to see to on the way there and back; also, before setting out, pay up all your debts.

It is never God's wish that any kind of injustice be involved in the doing of good works.

The most elementary justice consists in the avoidance of injustice.

Before all else, discharge your obligations to the Church, whose child you are. Do not act like many others who, in their desire to do good works, set aside the divine will; otherwise your works will have been of no avail, though you may not realize it.

Surely, God receives more gratefully the good you do

and the hardship you endure while on pilgrimage, when you have first done your duty to the Church. Indeed, in that case, every divine service you attend will benefit you.

[3]   When you would go to a shrine to pray, think it over in your heart, and ask yourself: 'What am I really after? I will not be saying anything important to this saint, nor is she likely to speak to me. O God, I would set out for this place in order to serve you, and finish the journey for the same reason.' With an attitude like this, you could stay home or go abroad, as you would.

Chapter Fifty

On the arrogance that scorns burial in a parish plot

[1]   It would be the height of pride if you—when death approached—were to spurn your parish cemetery, in favor of burial elsewhere. In so doing you would be disowning all the good counsel and care you received there where you sought to quit with sin and mend your ways.

[2]   When you set out for your own parish church, you are as high-minded as any pilgrim. What is more, you—like the poor who have little choice but to be buried there—will be fit to know God's tender mercies.

Chapter Fifty-One

Why God is wont to conceal the Mysteries from sinners

[1]   When sins are committed, it is by those who lack a ready faith. Each time you want to sin, the divine voice within you warns against it, saying, 'Do not do it!' But once you have undertaken to sin, you pooh-pooh all of conscience's rebukes. For those who are on the way to perdition[108] never believe either in the joys of Heaven or the pains of Hell, however much they may hear tell of such things, or read of them in the Bible, or have word of them from any source whatsoever.

God prefers to keep his foes in ignorance of his mysteries, just like any ordinary person would keep secrets from ill-wishers whom he may one day have to fight.

[2]   As it pleases him, the Lord strengthens his faithful ones in their faith and their love of goodness: some more, some less. When, however, faith and love seem to have deserted you, at least remember that these were yours once, and—if you keep away from evil—God will lead you back to them.

Chapter Fifty-two

On those who receive their good things now[109]

Nothing could be worse than that you should have had all your good things in this life; nothing better than to have had all your misfortunes already. Those who received all their good here on earth had it only as long as their journey through life lasted. Thus the difficulties they will have to sustain in eternity will prove all the more burdensome. Those who have journeyed through hard times, though, will take greater joy in the good they will receive, and will be well-pleased with all the labors they have endured for the sake of abiding repose. It is as Abraham said to that rich man who lay in torment: 'Son, remember that during your life you received good things, while Lazarus received bad; now he is being comforted and you are in torment'.[110]

Chapter Fifty-Three

A subtle case on Judgement Day

At the very moment when all people are raised for final judgement, one of God's elect will die, still needing to be purified of sin. But how can this now be achieved?

God is not dependent on the passing of time to make a sinner fit for Heaven. In a single instant God can mete out a chastisement that will do the work of a thousand years of Purgatory's fires. For, in truth, God is able to accomplish more than we can ever express or even think up.[111]

Chapter Fifty-Four

The fool is troubled for nothing

[1]   The fool is bothered by the sight of a Bonhomme keeping still in one place, occupied with no other thing. But bear in mind that a farm laborer is seen repeating the same action over and over upon his paltry plot of land, and no one would call him lazy for that. Then why think the like of someone who is sitting quietly with God in meditation—walking with God, as it were, through Heaven and earth—as if this was no real work at all?

[2]   Be it ever so narrow a place, a Bonhomme can tarry there with room to spare, because Love is his companion. But that fool who nurses resentments, all the world's kingdoms together will be too strait to hold him.

Chapter Fifty-Five

Intention Means Everything

[1]   To know if a deed is for good or ill, it must be considered in the light of its intention. Take the case of Judas and the Jews; they did all they could to bring about the death of Christ. Although this death was to save the world, it would profit those men not at all, since their own motive was so wicked. On the other hand, no one condemned Peter and the other disciples when the Lord's death so depressed them, because their sadness was considered good.

[2]   Why is it that Adam is sometimes put at the foot of the cross in paintings of the crucifixion? He stands for all the good people who were waiting in the netherworld until Jesus' death would set them free. And greatly did it please Adam that this was at last accomplished; thus he is pictured waving his hands about for joy, in the direction of the Lord upon the cross. The Mother of God and Saint John the evangelist, however, who stand nearby, are painted with mournful looks; for them, the Passion (for all its saving effects) could give no pleasure whatever. Such is the ignorance of the living!

Chapter Fifty-Six

The meaning of Saint Paul's handicap[112]

The key to Saint Paul's inner strength was that handicap of his. As a rich young man keeps his treasure for himself,[113] safe and sound, shutting it up against any intruder, so too did God, out of love for Paul. Into Paul God put a treasure of wisdom, then locked it up and took away the key; and when Paul besought God for it, he was refused. For had God taken that handicap away, Paul's treasure would have surely diminished.

Chapter Fifty-Seven

Even if you cannot stop sinning, never give up doing good

The doing of good works is still quite appropriate for someone whose belief in salvation is waning. Being unwilling to give up some pet sin is no reason to leave off doing what good you can yet do. On the contrary, this you should do with even more energy, as if you were saying in your heart:  'My God, I am going to do this good deed, although I know for certain that if I were to die unexpectedly I would be forever lost on account of that habit of sin I still have. All the same, Lord, I will go on doing good, that you might give me a hatred for that sin of mine.' Seeing this faith of yours God will root out that besetting sin, and recover all the good you persisted in doing. But act as if you will be saved in spite of your sin, and you will have no hope of that whatsoever.

Hope is the expectation that God will save you for the good works you have done. If, though, you reckon you can save yourself by behaving badly, you will lose all hope of it.

Chapter Fifty-Eight

A FOOL WORKS HARD ON ILL-DOING

A fool put into a position of responsibility can do more harm on earth than can an invading army. Enemy soldiers will move on sooner or later, but a fool will wreak destruction for many a long day. Solomon was so right when he wrote, 'Woe to that land whose king is a schoolboy'.[114]

Chapter Fifty-Nine

Make a clean break with the world!

[1]   Every kind of sin offends God, but worst of all is when someone commits a sin while hoping to equalize things later by doing a good deed.

[2]   For example, say you decide to do the best thing you can think of—like leaving the world to become a monk, or some other heroic deed. Then, with this future deed in mind, you indulge in one of your habitual faults, just once more, saying in your heart: 'I am going to be giving up my sins once and for all'. So, by acting like one who rolls in the mud[115] when he really wants to take a bath, you make it impossible for God to bring you to real goodness. What you ought to do rather, is, as it were, wash your feet, so you might plunge clean into your bath.[116]

Chapter Sixty

On money-lending

[1]   Whoever has recourse to a moneylender is doing wrong and is, in fact, just as wrong as the lender. This is why: if you spend what you cannot afford on expensive luxuries—fancy foods, clothing, etc.—when you already have enough to live comfortably, you will end up needing the services of a moneylender. Both of you, though, will incur the same guilt before God, lender and borrower alike.

There is no need for anyone to be in want, provided they live simply.

One blameworthy deed sets another in motion; make a habit of spending your money before you have even received it, and you will be forever wanting for something.

[2]   The money-lending trade offers many ways to be wicked, but the worst of all its practitioners is the pawnbroker. An end will come to the life of a pawnbroker, and his children will have to inherit the pledges he held. This state of affairs will speak more eloquently than if the man had said, 'My child I am about to die. While I could, I fought hard against God, but that is not enough for me; by leaving you these pledges, I will carry on my fight through you.'

[3]   Thus it is by such a maneuver that even a dead mon-

eylender can, as it were, go right on putting his money out to interest (and whatever is received over and above the amount borrowed counts as such ill-gotten profit).

[4]   If your patrimony consists of the tithes in goods or land of borrowers, your father has bequeathed you nothing but sin; claim it, and you may as well have asked to inherit a place in Hell. But, beyond any doubt, this you would never actually do; spend but a second in that place, and you would not wish to repeat the visit—not for all the wealth in the world.

CHAPTER SIXTY-ONE

WHO IS TRULY WISE?

[1]   A wise person thinks before speaking.

A fool cares little about clear reasoning, and simply blurts out a reply to, say, news that someone has done a good work. He says, 'God certainly owes that fellow a debt of gratitude, for having done so much good, and for love's sake!' You idiot, how can you talk like that? As if God has anything to thank us for! Should he be grateful that we can see with our eyes, speak with our mouths, or go about on our two feet? It is the other way around. It is we who must be thankful for God's gifts of motion, language, and vision, and likewise for his empowering us for good works.

[2]   Can you see how stupid it is to say, 'They have done well for themselves, have not they?' in regard to persons who have vanquished their enemies, imprisoning some and killing the rest. It is a mistake to describe as 'doing himself a favor' someone who has parted ways with God, and got himself damned to boot! Would you not consider yourself dealt falsely with if someone robbed you of so much as one bit of your body? What, then, must God think of one who wholly destroys himself, body and soul?

Chapter Sixty-Two

About Justice

If you would possess goods in a way that is just, be sure that you buy only what you need. If, though, you are not ready to go that far, at least include extra bread in your expenses, for bread—more than any other item—is most often needed by the poor.

If at present you do not wish to leave behind all wrong-doing, then for now give up some percentage of it. This is a wise method of instructing any sinner who is not up to a thoroughgoing conversion. Show him how even a rogue can still do good works, and you will give him more confidence than excessive demands for perfection ever would.

Chapter Sixty-Three

God's soldiers on campaign

[1]   To keep from doing evil while in a job wherein much evil is done is immensely pleasing to God and it takes a prodigious intelligence. This is how it may be done. Say you are bound to serve the lord of your land, and he summons you for a campaign. If your will is to remain close to God, before you muster, say to him in your heart: 'Lord

God, I will go on this campaign, but I claim you as my leader, under whom I will serve, swearing allegiance henceforth to you alone. I will rout evil and pursue good, in my own camp as in my enemy's, in whatever way I can.'

[2]   Intending to proceed in this fashion you can set out, running out ahead of your troop, as if to engage the enemy single-handedly. When these come into view, you can scare them off, lest they be taken captive. If your comrades want to take prisoners, though, you will have to assist them. But, as God's man-at-arms you can later contrive to let your prisoners go, while seeing to it that no one is endangered thereby. So will you be a monk worthy of bearing around your neck a scutcheon declaring, 'To Caesar what is Caesar's, and to God what is God's!'

[3]   Every soldier-monk must beware never to give alms from his share of the booty. For it would only be further sin to give to the poor what one has already stolen from someone else. Now, it is certain that stealing of any kind is a wicked thing. But if the robber then gives the gains to the poor, he may delude himself into thinking he is now free of guilt and fit to meet God. This would be as though a man were to kill a child before its father's very eyes, and afterward bring him his child's blood to drink in a golden cup!

Pillaging is a greater sin than is simple thieving, for the first has a viler pride behind it.

CHAPTER SIXTY-FOUR

ON REVENGE

There is no finer way to be well-revenged upon your enemy than to rob him of his very motive for doing harm. If you pay back evil with evil, your foe's store of malice will only be increased. By such doings, nobody settles a score; on the contrary, the account becomes even more unbalanced. If you have given your enemy more than you have taken away from him, you can hardly be said to have had your revenge! But repay an evil deed with a good one, and your revenge is complete,[117] for you have thereby invaded the very soul of your foe, and made off with a store of malice. The way is now open for that soul to repent; failing that, she will owe a more hellish debt after death, when vengeance is inescapable.

Chapter Sixty-Five

'Before you offer your gift at the altar . . .'[118]

[1]   The Lord says in the Gospel, to any who would make a sacrificial offering: 'If you are offering a gift at the altar, and remember your brother has something against you, leave your gift there at the altar, and go first and make up with your brother'.

This saying can be interpreted in two ways. Should you ever hurt someone, it is only just that you seek to put things right between you. Nor have you done anything exceptional in that; nay, you would be guilty of sin if you failed to act.

[2]   When, though, it is yourself who is the injured party—and by someone who meant to hurt you—then you will have done an outstanding thing if it is you who seek to make peace. This is what Jesus Christ himself did when he was on the cross; before they ever besought him, Jesus forgave those who crucified him. For this reason we can be certain that he, through the Gospel words, both counsels and wills that we should do likewise.

[3]   Another variation of this story would be if you were to hurt someone, and later ask for forgiveness, but the

other person flatly refused to forbear. In a case like this, God will apply whatever penalty your original offense deserved to the person who would not forgive it you. He, moreover, need not bother asking God to grant indulgence for any other sins either, seeing how unwilling he is to forgive another's offense.[119]

Chapter Sixty-Six

Take care how you treat the demented

[1]   It could happen to anyone to be seized with a violent headache, so bad that it distorts the senses and causes its victim to lash out with curses and oaths, unaware as he is of what he is doing or even of who he is at that time. Now, what if this person dies of this attack? And what if this same soul, prior to this illness, had always been law-abiding, keeping away from evil and clinging to God? It is unthinkable that he will be condemned for those oaths. For God is faithful, and will judge him by what he was like before that fatal illness.

[2]   It is highly recommended, for those prone to mental disturbance, that they be kept away from shrines and holy places, unless this is unavoidable. For the other pilgrims there are liable to laugh at such affliction, and so forget to attend to their prayers. Indeed, they may even torment such persons, only intensifying their confusion, making

the illness even worse, and those responsible would be guilty of grave sin.

The best thing is for a deranged person to be housed separately, in an out-of-the-way place, kept comfortable in all weathers, while his friends pray for his recovery.

Chapter Sixty-Seven

How silly for lay folk to criticize the clergy!

[1]   Sometimes lay people, wishing to justify their own sinful behavior, say: 'The clergy know the scriptures and the mysteries of God, so why do they commit sin then?' The wisest answer to such a question is the following: 'My friend, since you are aware of a cleric's sins, that makes you superior in insight; why, then, cannot you yourself avoid doing those things you criticize him for? God has written on your heart the scripture[120] that will always show you what you should do or leave undone; so if you sin, you do so as knowingly as any cleric!'

[2]   You know full well that you will never make any progress if you follow on behind someone who is on the way to destruction.

An imbecile of such magnitude is not to be found on earth who would say to his priest, 'I demand that you lead me to Hell forthwith!'

Chapter Sixty-Eight

A piece of good advice

[1]   Often people bewail situations they are never likely to be in, or fear giving what God is not asking for anyway, while leaving undone that which their situation demands. And so we hear it said: 'I lack the means with which to do great things for God, or even enough to give alms with'.

[2]   A wise counselor, though, can show the worrier wherein lies true wealth by enquiring: 'Now my friend, if you are all that poor, at what price would you yield up one of your feet or some other part of your body?' and will come the reply, 'Not for any sum!' Then, 'How large a fortune would you require for your eyes to be taken from you?' and 'So large a fortune could not exist', is the answer. The sage can then rejoin with: 'Why, you must possess immense riches then, since you refuse to part with what you have, even for great wealth!'

Take great care of your limbs, but with the sort of respect that will also preserve them from the eternal flames.[121]

Chapter Sixty-Nine

How religious who are wronged should behave

[1]   When someone brings evil upon a religious community, which in turn invokes God, pronouncing curses upon its persecutor, it is as if it forbade the Lord to see to it that justice is done. God (to whom vengeance rightly belongs)[122] would respond to their actions saying, 'Since you have not waited for me, but have taken your own revenge by those curses of yours, I will withdraw and leave you to it'.

[2]   To effect real justice, one would have to meet with the doer of the wicked deed and find out why it was done in the first place. If destitution is found to have been behind it, then the dispensation of the Church will come to his aid; but if the deed was done for self-aggrandizement, let the whole community beseech the Lord with one heart that the malefactor be forgiven.[123] Then God can either bring about a conversion, or else see that a penalty is meted out without further delay.

Chapter Seventy

No one, high or low, may leave the enclosure in order to pray

[1] A superior may send one of the community any-where, for the sake of the Order. But should you decide to take off, even for Jerusalem or some other holy shrine, in order to pray, you undermine all the good offered to one who enters a monastery. Furthermore, you would not be able to lay your hands on funds—given long ago to oth-ers—unless you are prepared to steal them. And finally, how will you who have, so to speak, cut off your feet, travel to Rome or anywhere else?

[2] When a whole community, with their superior, con-dones the exit of a rebellious member, it is obvious they were not satisfied with one apostasy, but had to go on to implicate the entire group in the sin. But the rebel will proceed toward Hell all the same, though unwittingly now, thinking the sin has been absolved. Had the community formally shunned the culprit from the start, he might have taken fright and repented.

[3] If a superior travels abroad for some pious purpose, the implication is that all may do likewise, thus the whole ideal of enclosure is undermined.

Chapter Seventy-One

Listening to the Divine Word

Whenever you listen to our Lord speaking in the Gospel, even if you cannot retain it all, let that much be enough for you; despise this portion, and you are sure to fall away. You must strive, at least, to hold on to so much that you are sustained until you hear God speak again, as when you sit down to meat and take enough to last you until the next meal.

Your soul needs to eat, just as does your body; neither can live long after its food is cut off.

Chapter Seventy-Two

The hows, whats, and wherefores of doing good

[1]   Many examples might be brought forward of how to measure a good action . . .

For instance, there is 'Goodness by subtraction', which is a kindness brought about not by positive effort, but simply by holding back on something.

'Goodness by addition' is an open-handed deed, which also gives pleasure and enjoyment.

'Goodness by multiplication' happens when a full compliment of goodness is accompanied by regret that one could do no more.

The last sort of goodness—'Heaped up, shaken together, and overflowing'[124]— is what we, whose freedom cost our Lord his life's blood, should give him in our turn.

[2]   Pleasure magnifies a wicked act just as it does a good one. This is why you would be guilty of a greater sin if you were to murder an enemy rather than a friend. For upon slaying a friend your self-loathing would be such that God would take it for heartfelt repentance, and forgive you. Whereas slaying an enemy would give you so much satisfaction as to put you beyond the scope of any forgiveness, on judgement day you would still be saying in your heart: 'Blessed are you, O God, who even now awaits my repen-

tance, but still it is a great pleasure to me that that wretch who sought to harm me is dead'. And with thoughts like this you could not be further from repentance if you tried.

[3] Repentance means being sorry for something you have done. It is a disposition that comes only by God's loving favor.

Before your priest makes a judgement about your sin, he asks whether you are sorry, or if it bothers you, to have done such a thing. Should you reply, 'It does not bother me in the slightest', what judgement can he make but that you have still to repent? If you say, 'I am sorry', though, the priest can confirm that God has gifted you with penitence, and absolve you so that you might go from that place a changed person.

Chapter Seventy-Three

It is harder work to be mediocre than to do great deeds
of goodness

[1]   Those who do a middling amount of good have a harder job of it than if they had aimed for great goodness. Run-of-the-mill benevolence never brings with it that perfect love of God in which we find our rest,[125] whereas great deeds will bring us into it.

[2]   How can you tell a great good deed from an ordinary one? It takes a doer of the former to see the difference; those who do the latter are not ready for such knowledge. But say you enjoy doing a good work, and can remain peaceful until it is accomplished; that would be a 'great good deed'. If, on the other hand, what you do gives no pleasure, and its doing upsets your peace of mind, what you have there is a small, common sort of good action.

Chapter Seventy-Four

The troubles and joys of this life

The wicked weep when they are angry and anxious, but when the good cry it is for joy and sweet affection.

The wicked have no wish to die and leave the troubles they have now, fearing they will only have it worse down below. But good folk long to pass on, from their present well-being to the greater blessings they hope for.[126]

Each of us will have a chance to know the joy of sharing laughter with God—a just outcome, seeing how much there was to cry about in our present lives.[127]

Chapter Seventy-Five

What distinguishes an upright person
from a worthless one

[1]   In many respects a bad person is like a good one. Both of them can keep vigil, fast, give alms, and all sorts of other things like that. But only the good person can forgive from the heart; a bad one cannot.

[2]   If it were demanded of some hugely-rich man, 'Hand over a penny, or you will die', he can easily comply and save his life. But say to a pauper, 'Pay a thousand marks of silver, or you will hang', and hanged he will be, for he cannot pay what he does not have. So it is with a good person, who is so abounding in goodness that forgiving from the heart is no burden, so filled with tenderness as to grant pardon before it is even asked for. A wicked person is so poor in goodness that to believe in—let alone accomplish—what goodness can do is quite impossible.

[3]   There are people who, on account of pride, spurn any pardon offered them by the upright, and say, 'I care nothing for your forgiveness'.
   If you show forgiveness to someone unwilling to accept it, it is as though you were scattering hot coals over the head and shoulders[128] of one whose haughtiness and scorn can only increase the pains of his hell.

CHAPTER SEVENTY-SIX

WHAT WOULD YOU SUFFER FOR?

[1] We shirk our duty toward God at such a very great cost! For he wants us, who have received his gift of faith, to put up with our troubles in this life and so make up for the times we have failed him. He has even joined his own sufferings and death to ours, for our redemption's sake. And yet, for those bent on their own destruction,[129] that death does no good whatsoever;[130] it even magnifies their debt. Not for these to bear the kinds of hardship that God would accept for their sins! No, they sin all the harder, and stand ever more aloof from good folk. So you can see how sins mount up—while those of sinful bent lose the very fear of any punishment.

[2] God is so faithful that he would liefer have us ask great things of him than small ones.

Ask God for a paltry thing, like worldly riches for instance, and sometimes you will be refused. Ask for something of consequence, like God's kingdom, and you ask well, for this he will surely give you.

To draw you toward something more, God may withdraw a lesser thing from you.

[3] If you submit with calm and good grace to lacking the bare necessities, you do well, though this is not yet

perfect self-control. There is a perfect sort of self-control that, having the object of the body's desire there before it, still leaves the thing untouched. But when even your taste for the world's pleasures has grown dull, then you possess consummate self-mastery.

CHAPTER SEVENTY-SEVEN

THE MEASURE OF GOOD AND EVIL

[1]   In every great good lies the risk of great ill. For the more familiar God is with you (and this, surely, is an immense good), the more serious it would be should you ever be at odds with him.[131] This is why the Devil's sin was so grave, because he knew the Lord so well. The same applies to the sin of Adam, who was made to exist amid so much goodness. So too with any of us, to whom God has given with such largesse of his benefits, material and spiritual; to then fall out with God would be a grave insult to him.

Here is something to instill a mighty fear in us all. By a single wicked thought, the prince among the benevolent angels was transformed into Satan, fallen for all eternity. What, then, of us, who are daily busy with our wicked thoughts and doings?

[2]   Let a scoundrel do a bit of good for a change, and he thinks himself a better man than someone who is always

busy with good works.

If you are a person of integrity, the more perfect you become, the less fuss you will make about your own goodness, though you hold it dearer than any other thing. This may appear to be a contradictory statement, but not if one understands it in the following manner: those who struggle and strive to be of use to the Lord in the doing of good will tend to belittle what they have accomplished, for compared with the ideals held up to them by the Holy Spirit, they know how much more could be done and see just how inadequate they are to the task.

[3] The Lord, though he loves us dearly, sees to it that the good we do seems shabby to us, lest he lose us. If you cannot understand this, you cannot have experienced the love of God overmuch.

CHAPTER SEVENTY-EIGHT

THE GIFTS OF GOD ARE DANGEROUS THINGS

[1] Those who have taken up monastic life have a greater dread of being called to account for God's unique gifts to them now, than for any misdeeds they may have committed when in the world. For we are all well aware of the fact that, if we have renounced our crimes, and for good, they are forgiven us. But in the case of our personal gifts, there are many ways we can squander these. For example, we

might despise others, or consider our good qualities as having originated in ourselves, or even that we have deserved these things; or again, we could imagine that our salvation is somehow assured by the gifts we possess. Finally, a craving for praise or material gain may cause us to rob God of any credit for what we are, though it is his due.

[2]   The many advantages God has bestowed upon us in the Scriptures and the Church's Sacraments can bring us condemnation, too, if ever we approach them unworthily.[132]

That bogus Christian, who both abuses good things and does evil ones, will be liable to a more severe sentence than will an unbeliever who has simply done wrong.

[3]   Should the Lord shield you from every ambush as you advance toward goodness, your gratitude and admiration for him will exceed anything you felt when he forgave you the misdeeds of your past.

Even the divine forgiveness can convict you, unless God defends you, if you behave like that servant in the Gospel who refused to forgive his fellows.[133]

God is such a wise custodian of his good gifts. He never allows them to be adulterated with anything evil.

Should you ever come forward to claim the credit for God's gifts to you, he will leave you there, in the clutches of his enemy.

Chapter Seventy-Nine

Brother Fool and Brother Wise in conversation

BROTHER FOOL: It would be enough for me if I could be a monk for the last year of my life, just so that at the end the Lord might find me busy doing good and proclaiming my faith in him.

BROTHER WISE: And do you also want the Lord to expel you from his presence after a thousand years? Or would you rather he saved you forever?

BROTHER FOOL: Oh, the latter, please!

BROTHER WISE: Well, if it is God's limitless salvation you want, and without end, how can you put limit or term to your service of him?

Chapter Eighty

Do not put off your quest for holiness

[1] It is the height of stupidity to put off confessing your sins, praying, and giving alms until the very end of your life. If you have been contending with the Lord for thirty or forty years, you can hardly expect instant forgiveness from God. You should at least be willing to foster friendship with him with as much sustained energy as you formerly spent in opposing him. It takes no time at all to stain your hands, but much longer to wash them clean.

[2] No work will ever demand of you as much energy and independence of spirit as will the work of prayer and wholehearted loving. When your body wears out and your mind begins to fail, how good will you be at relentless prayer and fidelity? When you are enfeebled with age it will take more effort simply to open your eyes than it took to be on the move all day when you were young and strong. Now, you are not being honest with yourself if you then say, 'If I was not so ill I would be at prayer before God'. To one who would do well in this situation, the Lord says this: 'Why rely now on your own prayers, when you have me? I am still here with you,[134] carrying out my duties on your behalf.' If, though, your motive is to get out of having to pray, God's word to you is: 'Well do I know how you

would behave should your health return!'

[3]   It would be a shame if, at your end, you still had the wherewithal to give even a single alms, and so protect yourself beyond the grave. It would have profited you more had you done the deed while you were yet healthy, rather than trusting others to give that sum in a piecemeal fashion after you die—others who, after all, could never love you as much as you loved yourself.

[4]   Foolish indeed are you who want all that you possess to be in good order in every detail, and then care so precious little about keeping clear of evil. You act as though you would give notice regarding your soul (the very orderer of all that you are): 'Go find your own protector!' and expose her to the power of the Enemy.

Chapter Eighty-One

Be in a hurry to do good

[1]   Whenever, and at whatever stage of our lives, we turn to him, God is well-pleased by it. But God is never better pleased than when a young person, bursting with energy and passion, withdraws from that mischief proper to youth, devoting those powers to goodness instead. This is to become that 'living sacrifice, pleasing to God'.[135]

[2]   Make haste and do good while you may, for once you let a chance to pray or be of service pass you by, you will never get it back—any more than you could bring back time that has passed.

Not only will we have to answer to God for our needless thoughts, vain words,[136] and wicked deeds, but also for the good we might have done when we were busy committing evil.

Neglect to do what you know would please God, and you have sinned like any felon. And futhermore, you will not be able to make amends for that sin unless God, by his free gift, forgives it you.

CHAPTER EIGHTY-TWO

NO MATTER HOW HARD WE ARE TRIED, GOD IS THERE

[1]   There may come a time, when you are at prayer, that some serious temptation takes hold of you, so that you cry out, 'Lord God, help me!' whereupon the temptation  grows even stronger. But then your Lord makes this interior reply: 'I am right here, helping you; the more violently you are tempted, the better I can support you through it. For I will not allow you to be conquered by temptation,[137] any more than I would let you wear the victor's crown if you won it by cheating. Until you have battled through to the end, let that thought comfort you, and admit how much you have need of me!'

[2]   God is faithful,[138] and would never load his beast so heavily (regardless of how strong it looks) that the weight might break its back. Nor would he beat it until it collapsed. No, God's only wish is to lead it back onto the road where it can progress more swiftly.

Chapter Eighty-Three

More about temptations

Persons of integrity will feel temptations more keenly than others, and for a reason: not because they think viler thoughts than the rest of us, who are content to be led about by our evil wills. Rather, the better they are, the more offensive any wicked thought will be to them. And the blame they take upon themselves for such thoughts will always far exceed what those who act upon the same would ever accept.

Chapter Eighty-Four

Temptations again

[1]   God is just as pleased whether we are reveling in spiritual sweetness or enduring temptation. Consider the following illustration of this. A married man must be away from home for a time, and while he is gone another man makes adulterous suggestions to the lonely wife. If she spurns the offer, her husband, on returning, is hardly likely to love her any less for that. In fact he will love her even more, for defending her virtue. And she, for her part, will

be so very happy to have him home!

[2]   If a company of knights defend their fortress from an enemy attack while their lord is away, upon his return he will be well-content when he hears how they stood their ground. Think, then, how great will be their gladness when they welcome him home! So it is with God, who is well-content when we defer the joy of his company, and embrace our time of trial.

Chapter Eighty-Five

When a Good Thing is Not a Good Thing

[1]   There are occasions when it can be a better thing to step back from a promised good than from some threat of evil.

No 'Bonhomme' needs to be told, 'Avoid killing anyone' (or some other crime), for if he is truly 'bon' he will be as careful of this as he can be.

[2]   The one who guides you in your spiritual life has the duty to see that you grow in humility, and so when you have done a good work, you may well hear: 'You could have done better'. Criticism like this is meant to detach you from the good you do.

Chapter Eighty-Six

Learn to appreciate humility

[1]   There is not a sinner among us whom God would not restore to moral health, if only that person would admit from the heart to being sinful; this is what makes humility such a boon.

Since God, in forgiving, will thereby reduce the sinner's store of evil, it follows that he will add increase to the virtues of the righteous too.

If it is so that God takes so much pleasure in the humble return of the sinner, then must he be especially happy when the upright make nothing of their own goodness.

[2]   Pride, when it finds its way into good folk, destroys the virtues they have gained. No wonder, then, that it makes bad folk even worse.

[3]   If God has given you the time and abundant help you have needed to live a long and loving life, then you should be well-content.

I do not doubt that were a villain to have just one day like yours to show at the end of his life, he would be saved.

Faithfully live each day in pursuit of God's kingdom and your reward will be great; all that the wicked will have acquired will be their places in Hell.

Chapter Eighty-Seven

Remembrance of sins past

[1]   There will be times in your monastic life when you will get insight into the sins you committed while still in the world. Then you will own up to them with tears, and pray God to unburden you of all your guilt. But when the warm glow of piety begins to fade, you may well discover you are still quite fond of those many and varied sins which you only today so bewailed. Though, now you have done penance for them, you may not actually commit them. So, now you can see something of the plight of the sinner still living in the world, where hearts are so opposed to God's will.

[2]   Self-mastery is one thing, self-defeat another!
Crush your vices underfoot, and you rise above yourself; to allow those vices to lay you low is self-degradation.

Chapter Eighty-Eight

Among the things we will marvel at in Heaven

[1]   Among the benefits we will marvel at in Heaven will be this: all of the elect will have an equal place there. No matter when you were born, or when you died, none will have precedence over you; nor will any who arrive after you be considered late. Then we will see the places in the Kingdom of Heaven assigned to us by Divine Providence[139] before the world ever came to be.[140]

[2]   In Heaven we will know what joy we have lost through our sins, and later have that joy restored to us by God's Favor.

We will sing the Lord's praises as much for the endlessness of salvation as for its having no starting point in his eyes.

Chapter Eighty-Nine

Regardless of our state at the end, each of us will give honor to God

[1]   God will get his honor from both the elect and the reject. Think of it this way. Two empires have a battle, and one ruler wins and imprisons the other. The victor will get as much honor by defeating his enemy as by the size of the reward he lavishes upon his soldiery. Likewise, God will have praise in the chastisement of some and the salvation of others.

[2]   God's mercy will be made manifest even in those who are on the way to destruction.[141] Manifest not to them, but in them, for others' sake.

One destroys a ruthless malefactor, and in this destruction lies a great mercy done to his potential victims. In a like manner the Lord does a merciful deed on behalf of his elect by moving the rejects so far away that they will never cause the elect any distress.

When the time came for him to withdraw bodily from his disciples, Jesus Christ showed his mercy by removing Judas from their midst. For they would have been distressed beyond all measure had he remained with them. While God was bodily present with the group, he allowed Judas to accompany them and handle their expenses (preoccupation with the nothingness of money being a fit job for a thief) leaving the others that much freer.

Chapter Ninety

The ways of the divine mercy

[1]   Blessed are you when none but God and you yourself see your own sins; this is one of the superlative mercies of God. He rarely rids you of any of your moral flaws totally while you live on earth. Rather he covers them, like one covers embers with ash, so that only you and he perceive them. If you are a servant of God, knowing your sins are still with you will produce conflict within, and this disharmony is the first step toward inner peace.

[2]   It is for love of his people that God puts some good in each of us. So when others praise you, it should not affect you in the least, for in truth, all the credit belongs to the Lord.

If we could see each other's thoughts, no one would be considered good.

[3]   Often something is seen where it is not, and unnoticed where it is. You might see a person's body engaged in doing good, though their heart be not in it. So, consider it a huge kindness shown you if God keeps you ignorant of other's thoughts.

Chapter Ninety-One

The discontent we show toward the mercy and justice of God

[1]   We are as little pleased with God's idea of mercy as we are by God's idea of justice. Only let a shameless individual be found living in a locality, and the people round about start asking: 'Why does God allow this? Such wickedness ought not to be tolerated!' But, you who think yourselves so wronged by this, what would you say if *you* were the object of such complaint? Or have you never done anything foolish in *your* life? And if you have, how would you like it if God were to leave *you* to your own ruin? You would not? Well then, since it suits you when God puts up with you, why must you complain when that same mercy is shown to someone else? While you are right not to take pleasure in human malice, you ought to be able to take pleasure in the sheer wonder of God's compassion, and praise it from your heart.

[2]   On the other hand, though, it seems that God's brand of justice affords us little pleasure either. We can be sure of one thing: we ought to love God more than anything or anyone. Whoever cannot manage that should at least acknowledge the constant love that they themselves receive from God. And if even this is not possible, let those for

whom it is not take great care not to *complain* about being so loved! Now, of course someone will protest: 'Being loved by God would never give me anything but pleasure!' But I would answer such a person thus: Whenever you are annoyed by the way God has ordered things (wanting you perhaps to endure continuing illness or poverty) so that by these trials you might at least desert your evil ways and learn to do good, I say that whenever such situations annoy you, then you have fallen away.

[3] You can see how supremely necessary this quality of character is, that with an honest heart we want all that God sees fit to do and say to us, finding fault with nothing. The fact of the matter is that it should be our own doings that give us little pleasure, seeing how futile they can be; whereas God's deeds produce such good effects, and are so worthy of our praise.

[4] Truly, if you do not realize this, you have yourself alone to blame when your sins trip you up, because you lack such fundamental understanding. Nor, in that case, will you be any better at learning that you too are a sinner, since you have no insight into God's motives which are as clear as day to most folk.

CHAPTER NINETY-TWO

THE GREATNESS OF DIVINE MERCY

[1] When God shows mercy to anyone, the very same kind of compassion is being shown, whether its object be one who has lived long years in doing good, or a sinner who has just turned to God at the end of life. If you question this state of affairs and insist that a sinner, who has never bothered to labor at a good life, must then be more tenderly loved by God than the decent person who has worked hard to be so, I will answer you in this way: If you have been enabled to live a dutiful sort of life all these years, you do not merely have an equal share with the sinner in God's compassion, but yours is a greater share. For had you not been held safely in the hands of God, be quite sure that you would have fallen into the same sins, perhaps sinking even lower!

[2] Where wrongdoing is concerned, we are all infected with the same rot. So then, if you are one of the favored ones who were not only made whole, but for whom moral goodness has long been a source of joy, consider yourself *twice* as tenderly loved by God. Is it not a greater advantage, therefore, to be able to endure the fire and heat of any passion without being burnt thereby, than it is to have escaped the fire altogether? After all, you were given a cer-

tain freedom from your sinfulness, while others will have to suffer for theirs, either in this life or in the fiery purification of death.

[3]   Here is another token of compassion which turns out to be a greater favor for those whom God saves early in life. The more upright your life, the more intense will be your felt need and desire for the wholeness God alone accomplishes. Indeed, God can more lovingly care for those who know their need and poverty (when they choose it) than for any who think they need nothing. It is a mark of a genuinely shameless person to experience neither aspiration nor interest toward receiving salvation; whereas one who is dutiful can be heard sighing and weeping when that grace is yet far off. When this is so, God, with the tenderest pity, fulfills that desire.

Chapter Ninety-Three

The unfathomable depths of God

[1]   The riches of God's mystery are so deep[142] that were we to know nothing more than that Scripture reveals to us a God who—from his abode in Heaven, and in this single moment—keeps every detail of this world in mind, we would be more zealous in his service. More zealous than we had ever been for the sake of what God has done, and does every day, for our salvation!

[2]   God has said it: 'Those who have labored in my service I shall give endless salvation'. But there are some who will retort: 'Then tell us, Lord, what is your will?' knowing full well that they will hear no locutions, nor personal messages through a third party. Then they fancy they have an excuse when, in their pride, they choose to sin, for they will say: 'Had we but known such doings were displeasing to God, we would never have misbehaved so!' But of course God never hides his will from anyone. At first he announced it through patriarchs and the prophets; then God came to earth in person and spoke to our deepest heart concerning the divine will; later, there were the apostles and other spiritual teachers. Moreover, God communicates his will to each person's conscience, giving us the power to distinguish good from evil.

[3]   In fact, the things God bids us do are so pleasant in their doing that had God not required them, we should have had reasonable cause to petition him saying: 'Lord God, this mutual love and living together in peace will be such an easy matter. Pray, allow us to do it!' So, when God goes further and commands it, would not anyone refusing to comply be deserving of a great, even severe, penalty?

Chapter Ninety-Four

What it means to receive the Body of Christ

If you are wanting to partake of the Eucharist, it is only reasonable that someone says to you: 'So you wish to receive the Body of Jesus Christ? and that God would surrender himself totally to you? If this is what you really want then God is ready to make that complete gift of himself, provided that you enter into a covenant whereby you undertake to give yourself to God just as completely.' Be honest. Is God making an excessive demand here? He is simply saying: 'Give yourself wholly to me, and I will give the whole of myself to you'.

What you give to God will be yours to keep. Even what you refuse to give him (everything you hold back) will belong to you in the Land of the Lost. Just as the Gospel says, the one who loves his soul will lose it[143] and whoever loses it[144] will gain it.[145]

Chapter Ninety-Five

Be mindful of your God

[1] Your waking, your working, and your settling down to sleep, all should be accompanied by a single intention. The voice of the heart should ever say: 'Defend me, Lord God, that I may not depart from you. Yesterday, it is true, I was not consistent enough in pursuit of my goal. Today I mean to redouble all my efforts to stay with you.'

Yes, bear in mind that one day you will die, but today you have been granted a stay of execution, so do what good you can, and you will be on the right foot, so to speak, to enter the next world.

[2] In your final illness, when you know your days are numbered, confess and do your penance, but then turn your whole heart toward the gracious support of Jesus Christ, and toward the love he bears each member of his Body. Then call to mind the main task God gave you to do, and all the help he gave you to see it through. With these memories of love-in-action, with faith, and with

hope in salvation, take your leave of this world.

[3]   To make a good death, one needs to have labored long at loving; even the courage to die comes only to those who have had an untiring care for justice.

No one who loves the Lord may ever desire death, but only long to see their Beloved.[146]

Chapter Ninety-Six

. . . AND THE GREATEST OF THESE IS LOVE

[1]   Genuine charity will have the greatest,[147] most perfect[148] reward in Heaven, for she has been the friend of God,[149] and could never belie that fact in her deeds. Of all the things her eyes light upon she always prefers the meanest: the shabbiest clothing, the least tasty food (just what is needful to hold body and soul together through the day), returning often to the inner chamber of the heart, there to contemplate her treasure,[150] Jesus Christ.

[2]   The prince of this world prizes a single farthing more than Charity values all earthly riches together, for she longs for a better home in Heaven.[151] One could even call her greedy, seeing that the whole world cannot satisfy her!

If you have Charity, what others say about you will not concern you in the least. Your dearest wish will be to keep yourself hidden from the world and unnoticed. Your sole object will be the perfect doing of God's will, and no fear of poverty or hardship will deter you from it.

Throw your self-concern away now, and the King of Heaven will see to it that every subject in his realm will admire your beauty.[152]

A friend of God can expect higher praise from the angels than can all the world's friends put together.

[3]   Nothing pleases true Charity more than God's com-

mand that she love her enemies[153] (in any case, it is more pleasant to love than to hate), and to have been bidden to pray for her persecutors[154] makes her even happier. Why, the Lord wants even torturers to receive his mercy, and wills that his friends plead on their behalf. And plead they do, in the knowledge that the Lord reserves his choicest mercies for those who suffer hard labors for him.

So, these are the thoughts and deeds of real charity. You may well ask, though: 'Is there anyone who could actually be like that?' Of course! This is the way by which Saint Peter and all the elect mounted to Heaven. And will anyone who is determined to love as much as those did—and longs as they did for salvation—not, to some degree, behave as they did as well? At least that much! Have no doubt, such is your duty. Believe that, and you will turn away from evil and do good[155] with all your might.

Chapter Ninety-Seven

Our graced relationship with Jesus Christ

[1]   If your heart's sole stay is the grace of Jesus Christ, you can be happy indeed; for if we could save ourselves by good works alone, Abraham and our other forbears of Old Testament times would not have had to go down to Hades when they died. But as things are, Moses and John the Baptist and those countless others who went down would have remained there forever, since only the Son of God could set them free.

[2]   If it were possible for all the good works of all the good people who have ever lived or ever will live, plus all the good that anyone left undone, to be credited to you, still, without God's gracious help you could not earn a single second's worth of the beatific vision.

The only return we can rightly claim from God for our own attempts at virtue is censure. Even if we have taken more pains than others to conform to God's will, in his opinion it would only be just enough to snatch you from the torments of Hell. This would be true even in the case of his own mother, for every human being shares in that sin into which we all have been born.

[3]   There is no better piece of advice any of us could hear than this: Wait upon the Lord and live for him as carefully

as you can. Then, whether your end is salvation, or not, you will have pleased him now. Even if you were absolutely certain that you were bound for Hell, that would not release you from your duty to serve God.

[4]   Considering that Jesus Christ has accomplished everything needful for human salvation, and that nothing is wanting for our sure deliverance (providing we stay clear of sin), why would anyone want to draw back[156] from his service?

God is faithful;[157] there is no cruelty in him. Yield yourself to him and he will save you.

God's deeds of goodness, he performs through us by his free gift; his salvation comes to us in the same way. From this same free gift God wants us to draw hope, for all the other wants we have. But if you spurn the first element in God's gift, that is, the doing of good, you will not be worthy of anything else, including salvation.

Chapter Ninety-Eight

How God will honor those who love him

God has many ways of showing honor to those who love him. The highest mark of esteem we will ever receive, though, is the salvation God bestows—not as a reward for any good deeds of ours, but by his own free will and gracious gift.

It could come to pass that a pauper might answer a royal summons, and receive some token of the king's esteem. But would it not be a greater expression of the king's respect if he were to travel abroad in search of the pauper, then bring him to court to sit beside the throne, appointing him lord of the demesne?

It would have been the same for the lost sheep.[158] She might have wandered home by herself, and unaided. But was it not a higher honor that the shepherd himself sought her out, hoisted her up on his own shoulders, and brought her back home?

God himself makes your salvation his special care. Could he do you a greater honor?

Chapter Ninety-Nine

Wickedness earns its own disgrace

[1] The wicked have no one to blame but themselves for the shame and disgrace they must bear; by their own free actions they condemn themselves.[159] What God wants is that we follow him freely, so that he can bring us to salvation. He has relinquished even the power to damn anyone; it is the individual who puts that power in his hands.

[2]

Do you find your delight in God? That is because
he delights in you.
Can you rest quiet in him? That is because
God can take his rest in you.
Is God your welcome guest? That is because
he already lives in you.

For God can neither rest, nor delight, nor live in what is not himself. If he could, that would mean that God was not the universal source of the goodness of all things.

Chapter One Hundred

Only the Lord can keep us safe

[1]   Seek your security in anything but God, and you will never find it.

Listen to the lives of saints and of people who have borne hard labors for the Lord. If you could ask them, they would tell you to do as they did (for what they suffered counted only for their own redemption). If you are unwilling to imitate such persons, their pains will serve only to terrify you.

[2]   Think of the lesser beasts, deprived of reason, who can do none other but be busy doing the Lord's will. This should awaken great shame and fear in your heart, that though privileged to have the use of reason, you shrink back from your part in God's plans. But act like this and you will end up being afraid of any and everything.

[3]   Only Jesus can say to one who holds him dear:

> All that I did, I did for you.
> For you I was born and baptized.
> My death is your life,
> my resurrection your forgiveness,
> my ascension your glorification.

It is God—who loved you more than any other, suffering willingly for your sake—who now keeps you securely. You will see. All else will fail you in your time of fear.

CHAPTER ONE HUNDRED ONE

QUESTIONS AND ANSWERS

[1] MONK: Brother Stephen, you are forever putting God's law before us on every possible occasion. Why, then, does the Lord command the children of Israel to despoil the Egyptians of their treasure, and bear it away when they depart?[160] This seems like stealing to me.

STEPHEN: The justice of this is as plain as day, Brother. The Israelites served long and hard under the Egyptians, and got nothing but evil as their wage. Now, God, who knows what is right and fair, made a just judgement: that those who worked (and were cheated of their wages) should take some reward for their toil with them when they moved on. In fact, this tale can have a spiritual interpretation, too, for the members of Christ received the treasures of the Holy Scriptures from the Jesus who stayed in Egypt, that is, in this dark world.

[2] MONK: Brother Stephen, you have often told us that God loves Jerusalem above all other places on earth. So much so that he arranges for his friends to come there (his virgin mother was even born there); the Scriptures frequently call it the 'Promised Land'. Do you not think it strange, then, that God did not make of Jerusalem a ver-

dant place of deep springs and rivers brimming with life?
Instead he leaves it a marsh land of burning heat (worse
than many other places) whose only water lies in pits dug
in the ground.

STEPHEN: (Soothingly) This, Brother, is precisely how you
can tell the divine plan is at work. And wonderful it is, too!
God sees to it that his friends can find no earthly delights
for themselves, so that his love for them will be their grassy
meadow, watered by springs and rivers, where they find
their sole refuge.

But even if God had known of a better world than ours,
he would never have brought us to such a place; still less
would he have deceived his mother with it!

[3]   For the sake of our future happiness with him in
Heaven, God deprives us of the joys of the present. Not to
neglect us and leave us here in misery; no, he wants to do
so much more for us—in the meantime giving us a deeper
peace, while worldlings think we are suffering hardship.
(And God deserves even more praise when he bestows such
repose in the midst of distress!) Sometimes, to confound
the faithless, he publicly displays in the midst of a martyr's
torments that aspect of sweet peace known only by his
friends. It was just so for the three youths who blessed God
from the fiery furnace.[161] As for those who have no relief
from their sufferings—so that the faithful might have examples of patience—God comforts them too, and mightily, but interiorly. But one day the torturers will suffer far
more than their victims ever did!

Chapter One Hundred Two

Our warm-hearted God

Our God is a gracious Lord. As often as we wish (though without demanding) to converse with God in prayer, he is there ready to listen. If, however, you presented yourself before some powerful personage of this world wanting to have private speech with him, chances are you would be kept waiting until another day.

Chapter One Hundred Three

Guidance everyone can use

Whoever would have free and easy conversation with God needs to understand that God cannot hear a summons that comes from a distracted heart. What friend could visit you if, after you sent the invitation, you went off on a journey? So, be careful that silly thoughts do not entice your heart away; rather remain therein as you pray, and God will be present to you.

Chapter One Hundred Four

Excerpts from a talk of Stephen's on prayer

[1]   (In answer to a question about aids to prayer)

When Moses prayed, he was wont to lift his arms Godward. For example, he did this when his servant, Joshua, did battle with Amalek. As long as Moses kept his hands aloft, Israel prevailed; but when he let them drop, the people lost ground. Finally, Aaron and Ur supported Moses' arms until their victory was complete.[162]

[2]   Then again, Mary Magdalen, when she came to the Lord, that he might forgive her sins, cast herself down at his feet. God pardoned her for the sake of the great love with which she was filled,[163] seeing she loved the Lord before ever she sought him out.

Thus Moses held his hands aloft in order to put more love into his prayer, and so improve it. Mary Magdalen achieved the same effect, but by lying at Jesus' feet.

So, when you are praying privately, find a position that suits you, that will increase your feelings of love for God—be it sitting or standing, humble prostration or kneeling.

[3]   However you do pray, be sure that humility attends your efforts, for without that your prayer is useless; God

will not listen to you.

When the holy disciples, James and John, besought Jesus for a favor, but without humility, he replied: 'Seats for you at my right and my left are not for me to give you; they belong to those to whom my Father has assigned them'.[164] By humility you can be the recipients of these places. Go ahead and be so, then!

The power of your prayer is measured by the strength of your love for God. But divine love cannot dwell in you unless humility makes room for it. So Jesus Christ promised the humble of the earth the highest dignity in the Kingdom of Heaven,[165] for he found no one else here who could love him.

[4]   There is a time and a place for every godly work,[166] but not in the case of prayer. There is a proper time for saying psalms, for talking about God, for listening to such talk, and for working; for all else it is the same. God has varied his requirements so we will not grow sick of serving him; instead we change from one activity to another with optimum enjoyment. But he wants us, in each and every thing we do, to pray to him, saying from the heart, 'My God, I do this so that I might love you'.

[5]   Whoever you are, whenever you take up a new action, God says: 'If you want me to, I will do this with you, and help you in whatever you purpose'. Now, someone with worldly aspirations will reply: 'Go help somebody else, not me!' This we may all say by what we do; that is, whenever we evade what God enjoins, and so reject his

companionship. God will then say: 'Since you care not to work in company with me, I will not be there to do your bidding either!'

[6]   There is a right way to do every deed, and God is best pleased when we keep to it. This is especially true of praying. The best way of doing this is as follows. Say you need God's help when you or someone else is in trouble. Pray then, but be ready to conform your will to God's. Never dare to choose ahead of time, nor dictate: 'Do it this way God'. Rather, put everything in his hands, to do with as he sees fit. This is God's way to pray; practice it and God will give you a favorable hearing. The same is true on the level of religious life; a faithful monk obeys his prior, and once having renounced himself nevermore chooses for himself.

[7]   When you come to a firm faith, you will praise God as much for what he denies you as for anything he grants you, be it material or spiritual. As God supplies one with wealth to serve him with, so he takes away another's wealth so that he might be better loved. And just as God deals out virtues to one as a help to salvation, he takes away another's as protection from pride.

[8]   Although everything to do with the common good should be of supreme importance, still, there will be times when you need to pray for a close friend, and you do well in this. But let this be your intention, that your friend may love God all the more.

The hungrier you are for something, the more ardently you will beseech the one who can give it to you.

However you do it, it is good for you to draw close to God and pray for yourself, for friend or foe, or for all of these at once.

Chapter One Hundred Five

Stephen's teaching on another matter

When asked why one reads in Scripture the words 'praise God' and 'bless God', when God needs no blessing from any human being, Stephen answered:

Scripture prescribes only what will be for our salvation. So, when it bids us praise or bless God, this is so that we might have the profit of it. For each time someone says with a sincere mind; 'Praise God!' or, 'Blessed be God!' straightway the Lord adds '... and for you who have praised me there will be praise!' or '... blessings upon you who have blessed me!' And God has good reason to respond like this, since none of us can bless him unless God has already bestowed a blessing. His gracious love makes the first move.[167] The original blessing from God, planted deep within you is a growing thing, so that when you bless God, this increases your capacity for God's blessing and love.

Chapter One Hundred Six

Praise surpasses petition in perfection

[1]   The more perfect sort of prayer is praise, rather than petition. When you praise God, you get the object of your longings there and then. And, too, you share—in your earthly way—the very ministry of the angels in heaven. Whereas, if you concentrate on asking for things from God, nothing gets settled, and you must continue in a state of uncertainty.

[2]   Live your life with integrity and love God at all times, and you will never need to ask him for anything; only praise him, and he will most certainly load you with more than you could ever think of wanting.

This thought often occupies one who lives wholeheartedly in the Lord, together with this interior prayer: 'Lord God what shall I ask of you? No one can ever conceive of all that you have done for your human creatures. For you have given yourself (and with this, all else) to anyone willing to receive you[168] and who longs to do your will.'

In this state of spirit, Bonhomme, praise will be your only prayer, for then no lesser needs will so much as cross your mind. Sadly, though, our weak human nature cannot remain always on this plane, and then we must pray for things again.

Chapter One Hundred Seven

Another question for the Master

[1] DISCIPLE: Whereabouts in the Bible can I find all those 'new songs'[169] that are forever being sung in heaven?[170]

STEPHEN: Look in the Gospel. Jesus Christ taught his disciples what this 'new song' is, when he said, 'I give you a new commandment: LOVE one another'.[171] He calls Charity that 'new song' because he makes us new, turning children of darkness into children of light.[172]

[2] Charity—the new song of the human race on earth—is the new song of the angels in Heaven, too. Whenever they see one of the elect ascend from earth to Heaven, they celebrate with a new song. But even when they have not this cause to sing God's praises, still, they go on rejoicing until the end time whenever a sinner repents, as the Lord says in the Gospel.[173] Seeing the Lord taking up the cause of another's salvation—and knowing that this person will stray no more—the angels make merry with abandon.

When the Son of God ascended into heaven clothed in flesh, the angels were amazed. They cried: 'Who is he, the King of Glory?'[174] And, now they have had this happy surprise, each time a part of the Body follows the Head into glory they will sing a new song.

Chapter One Hundred Eight

Goodness will be honored by God

[1]   God bestows many different honors upon those he plans to save.

We will be rewarded for all the times when, for God's sake, we refuse to do any of the evil deeds of which we are capable.

We will have God's praise and esteem when we reject our sinful ways and turn instead to him. In fact, the bigger sinner you were, the more the heavenly court will admire you. 'Look!' they will say, 'that one deserved the hottest place in Hell, but God—in bold combat with brilliant tactics—set the wretch free!'

[2]   Think of a soldier who is decorated, after the war is won, for the injuries he sustained in the defense against the enemy; and is praised, too, for fighting on, even after being wounded. God treats his friends in just such a fashion, honoring them for the virtues they exercised in defense of their souls, surrounded by pits of past sins while never falling to their damnation. These fulfill the Apostle's word concerning the Holy Spirit, who is working in all things for the good of those who love God.[175]

Though it is true that God is predisposed to show us mercy, and even honor, we must not consider this as leave to do evil,[176] but rather as a motive to make amends for sin and to hope for salvation through the good we do.

Chapter One Hundred Nine

A good life is a happy life

[1]   No spiritual treatise, nor sermon, could ever convey to you the happiness attending the Bonhomme's life. This you have to experience for yourself. Serving God gives him so much pleasure that even if he knew for certain he would never be damned, no matter what crime he committed, still he would keep clear of sin. The practice of virtue is his favorite occupation! Having already begun on earth the life of heaven, he frequently imagines how sweet it is going to be when he arrives in the Kingdom of Heaven, like a man coming home to his kin.

[2]   Think how a knight revels in the welcome he receives at court from the nobles who know him, when they rise from their places and bid him sit with them. So it could be for you, when you reach Heaven and the angels, recognizing in you their old comrade from the land of tears and sighs[177] who used to join in their praise of the Lord, now joyfully usher you in. This is the only recognition that matters to a Bonhomme; though he lack any other regard, for this, he will give his all to doing good.

[3]   Another way of imagining the event of your salvation is from the angels' point of view, as in this tale.

Once upon a time, a rich man betrothed himself to a woman. Then he gathered all his friends round him and told them of his plans to wed, and what date had been fixed for the feasting. While they sat on together he detailed the many sterling qualities of his bride-to-be, so that when she would arrive, his friends would welcome her with due honors. Meanwhile he sends word to her home, that she should start out for the wedding. (Oh, the naivety of the woman who would accept an apple from a stableboy, then spurn her fiancé's bridal gift and decline his invitation to join him!)

Now, the bride of Christ is the human soul, purified at the cost of Jesus' own blood.[178] His hall is our home above,[179] where he sits waiting for the soul, in the company of his friends, those already sharing his glory. While she is still here below, on earth, he sees to it that she is nourished, providing his own flesh and blood, lest she die of hunger. (And is it not foolish in the extreme for an unfilled soul to settle for a rotten apple here and now—a false existence, gained through a dalliance with the devil—in the process spurning the gift of Jesus Christ, the Robe of Charity,[180] for her to wear on her journey to him?)

A thirsty soul prizes the Robe of Charity[181] so highly that she would rather let her body be hacked up bit by bit, than ever to shrug off that garment. This is the reason why, when she arrives among the angels, they find her no stranger and show her deference.

Chapter One Hundred Ten

Of ruined angels and serene saints

[1] Although Heaven be the land of universal repose, Satan finds nothing but unquiet there, because he harbors such ill will against the God of Heaven. Whereas when Abraham and many others had to wait for a time in Hades, the land of torment, they felt no pain during their sojourn, for they were taken up with loving God.

Know that there is no rest except in loving God.

[2] It happens every day that wicked people find nothing good in the world, even when it is there. A Bonhomme, however, can find good even when it is absent. Here is how. When, in your service of God, you go in the name of Jesus Christ to the aid of some unsavory character, and treat him as if he were already good, insofar as you put your trust in him, you will discover his better qualities.

No matter how good you are, wicked folk will never see you as good, because they refuse to trust in the goodness of anyone. Judas, for example, would not even trust Jesus.

Just because you yourself are wanting in goodness, do not be too quick to credit someone else with it either.

If you are acquainted with a really good person who loves God mightily, do not be over-complacent in your esteem, for there is always room for improvement in everyone. This is because every good person is indwelt by God, whose goodness always goes beyond our present understanding.

CHAPTER ONE HUNDRED ELEVEN

THOUGHTS ABOUT SATAN

[1]   If you have ever wondered how it happened that Satan fell so swiftly from Heaven, this becomes obvious when you imagine how he would behave up there, should God permit him to return. When Satan marked that the Son of God was here below, on earth, and in the flesh, he murdered him.

[2]   As for the lost angels who followed Satan, they showed clearly by their actions that they were his. He was their leader, just like in the old days when they were all together in Heaven.

 We Bonhommes can join with the angels in praising the Lord for allowing the demons to live on in Hades, so that we might better appreciate the peace of Heaven.

Chapter One Hundred Twelve

The gift of the Holy Spirit

[1]   The reason why Jesus Christ did not give the Holy Spirit to the apostles while he lived with them on earth is because he himself consoled them; he was their 'Paraclete'. Had he given the Spirit then, as he did later, others of the faithful could draw this conclusion, saying: 'We will never possess the Holy Spirit as completely as the apostles did, since Jesus Christ is not living bodily with us, as with them'. Instead he sent the Spirit from Heaven on the day of Pentecost, so that thereafter we could always count on his presence.

[2]   When Christians do the works of faith, it is the Spirit who adds the savor to them all.

Pentecost can be called the spice of every other feast day.

However sweet we might find the singing of our offices, this is only because the Spirit breathes through them; otherwise they would taste of nothing whatsoever.

To be a friend of God gives a feeling of deep, intense sweetness. This shows itself in the ability to affect the spirit of others with one's charm, speaking words that sweeten sour dispositions.

Chapter One Hundred Thirteen

The feast of Pentecost is related to Good Friday, the day
when the Son of God was shamefully cast out of Jerusalem
bearing a cross on his back, on account of which the heavenly Father honors Jesus through the praise and witness of
his disciples. The acclamation of a single one of these is of
greater value than the dishonor shown him by all unbelievers put together. For surely it was by enduring such
disgrace that the Lord won so much praise. Patience works
like that, and deserves such response.

Chapter One Hundred Fourteen

Good and evil are not equal forces

The greater the good deed, the more satisfaction it brings; the same goes for evil in this regard. But for every person who can lust hard after evil, there is another who can long for good even harder. An example might help you to understand. Nothing that sin can offer in the way of pleasure and possessions can entice someone to die willingly for another. Nor would a lover of God, receiving the threat, 'Desert God, or die!' hesitate to choose death and cling to God. See how the love of good will always outstrip the love of evil.

Chapter One Hundred Fifteen

How the Saints help us

I will explain how the Saints help those who call upon them. When you pray to Blessed Mary or one of the saints, the Lord will hear your deep devotion and see to your need. Then he will show the saint what has happened, saying: 'For love of you I granted this favor to your supplicant'. You must not believe that the saints bring God the latest news about your needs. If they know, it is because God has shown them. When it dawns on the saints what God has done for love of them, they praise and thank him, and gaze upon his mercies all together in an instant. They have no need to intercede, but only to praise and love God. It is as the psalmist said: 'They are happy who live in your house, Lord, forever singing your praise'.[182]

Chapter One Hundred Sixteen

The wages of goodness

[1]   None of us can know or praise God well enough in this world.

In comparison with God's real magnificence, I am tempted to say that everything that prophets, apostles, and saints have told us about him is well-nigh disgraceful.

God will give more to a single one of his chosen ones than can be grasped in all of the thoughts that will ever be thought or, still less, expressed.

Even in this present life, a Bonhomme can at times experience the bliss of God so keenly that he could never describe it, nor put it in writing.

[2]   We are not even able to understand or relate all that goes on within ourselves. How could we say anything of value about the depths of God?

None of us can—even after close examination—explain why it is that the mouth does not hear, why the eye speaks not, or why the ear does not see, when all three openings are in the same head, and are organs activated by a single spirit. So you are wise if you simply stand in wonder before what the power of God can do. The fool will not hear of such things as miracles.

Chapter One Hundred Seventeen

We will know the fulness of love in the Kingdom of Heaven

[1] Only in the heavenly Kingdom will we possess the fulness of Charity. There it will be complete, and each of the elect will love every other like another self,[183] while all will love that individual likewise in return. Then every citizen of Heaven—angelic as well as human—will turn toward the Lord, and love him more than their own selves.[184] God will not, however, be outdone. He will love each one with more love than everyone together can give one to the other and to God—more, really, than we can ever conceive of!

Just as a group of people can all look at the sun at once, without any blocking the others' view, allowing everyone a complete experience of it, so it will be in Heaven, where God will give himself wholly to each of his elect—not partially, but all at once.

[2] Ah, but we are so lazy. Of this you can be sure, though; should one of God's apostles accept to return to this earth and preach to its people, what crowds would gather then! Why, then, are not these crowds hurrying toward the Church, that place where all twelve apostles now dwell?

Make the effort to become well-versed in solid, spiritual teaching; so much so that your conviction influences your behavior.

Just as there is more pleasure to be had in eating honey than looking at it, so the Word of God affords more pleasure to those who act on it[185] than to those who only listen to it, or copy its letters, but never get around to doing it.

CHAPTER ONE HUNDRED EIGHTEEN

FILL YOUR MIND WITH THOUGHTS LIKE THIS

A Bonhomme does well to reflect from time to time about what it will be like in the Kingdom of God. Your consummate good, however, lies in applying your mind to how you should behave in this world, until you leave it.

You do well if you prevent a demon from conquering you, but this is not good enough, you must be the conqueror.

Keep clear of evil, and you deny a demon the chance of victory; keep others from becoming demon-thralls, and your victory is complete.

There is no viler perversity than wishing that someone would grow used to slack observance and end up suffering for it, rather than wanting him to persevere quietly in doing what leads to joy.

Chapter One Hundred Nineteen

God's compassionate love for Suzanna[186]

[1]   Great was the compassion God showed Suzanna, when he defended her from being stoned. But passing great was that tender pity that protected her from sinning by consenting to the will of those corrupt judges. Had she been stoned, though, but never sinned, she would have suffered no loss except in the eyes of the crowd. Had she been guilty of sin as well, she would have gained Hell for her trouble.

[2]   At first God had no need of help to act on Suzanna's behalf; the divine Spirit could touch her woman's heart directly. This was the greater deed of mercy, for it was worked deep within her. And, too, the first led to a second, which God worked with the help of Daniel. 'Go,' said God to him, 'and say to the Babylonians that Suzanna has overpowered them all, for she stuck to the truth, but they to falsehood.'

Chapter One Hundred Twenty

Would you want God to let you leave him?

[1]   No greater misfortune could ever befall you than that God would allow you to depart from him in peace.[187]

When his chosen ones think to distance themselves from God, he hedges them around with thorns, blocking their way,[188] lest they accomplish their perverse will.

There are some who have shown themselves to be moving away from salvation. Sometimes God lets them prosper, but when they die, greater will be their pains. To these it can be said, 'Depart from God in peace'; they can then pursue their evil desires without any interference from the Lord.

[2]   It is not surprising that the blind are apt to take the worst thing if given a choice among several.

Those who love this world have eyes only for what pleases the flesh. Lust shuts up their spiritual senses, and so they pick what is worst for themselves.

A Bonhomme with clear eye for good, and a trained arm, will choose the better thing.

Stand in the street at noon, when the day is at its most brilliant; if you fail to see the sunshine then it is certain that you will see nothing else either. It follows, too, that they are absolutely blind who do not perceive the clear radiance of God, who makes the sun to shine.

There are people who never think of God; neither do they value his commandments. This is because they cannot imagine that God is either mindful of them, or cares what happens to them. If they only knew how closely God watches all the mischief they plan and get up to, they would on no account do such things ever again.

Chapter One Hundred Twenty-One

Listen to God's Word!

[1]   There are persons who, though they hear the words of God proclaimed, fail to put them into practice;[189] for what they hear is not what God has called good, but what they want to do.

[2]   If what you want is to love God with all your heart,[190] you are bound then, to be better pleased by the news that someone else (and not you) has come into a rich inheritance, or got a high office, or a title useful in this world. What makes this possible is your conviction that it is others who have the superior knowledge in profit-making, good investment, and charitable donation. There is a more compelling reason yet; one ought always to prefer that others (and not you) be saddled with the spiritual impediments in the world that distance us from God.

Chapter One Hundred Twenty-two

A talk on tithes

Villain! You who steal God's tithes, listen now by what right and reason God claims his tenth part.

You dig up the earth, sow last year's seed in it; later you harvest and store its produce. All of this belongs to God, and this is why:

That land you work on is God's; the iron and wood of your tools are his. God gave you the beasts that help you in the fields. Who gave you the seed you plant? Who else but God? And after you sowed the seed and fertilized it, who do you think gives you something to harvest from it, if not God, who tends it with such care? He it is who sends your crops everything they require: the rain and the sunshine, the cold and heat.[191] His are the dew and the rime, as are the balmy breezes.[192] For each little grain in your fields God fashions a sheath to protect it while it multiplies. Finally, when the reapers arrive, what would you do if God did not send you more of his sunshine? And when you have gathered the crops, and set to threshing them, God must send you his wind to separate the grain from the chaff.

But if sevenfold (or at least more than you saved) is not what you end up with, you complain to God, and bewail the waste of your labors. It would seem a more just division, for God to receive the nine parts, and for the tenth to go to you, considering the extent of your contribution to the project!

But our God is so soft-hearted that he grants you the nine parts that are his by right, so that you can have all you need. So give God his tithe; hold it back and all you have will be ill-gotten.

CONCLUSION

To those who are curious about our way of life, we
respond as Stephen taught us.
He supplied us with many replies saying . . .

Brothers, it should come as no surprise that certain persons
disagree with your way of life and customs. After all, you
disagree with their ideals, and have no wish to follow them in
what they do, so why should their opposition shock you?

There is never a need to ask other religious which Rule
they follow. The habit worn by each tells us: this one lives
according to Saint Augustine's Rule, that one follows the Rule
of Saint Benedict. And so, many will say to you: 'What is this
fad you have taken up? No doctor of Holy Church has de-
vised it'.

Those who interrogate you may bear the habit and trap-
pings of a religious, but I will have you know—and upon my
word—they are playing false to their own observances, because they have no insight into what Orders and Rules really
are. So, answer them this way: 'If there is something blameworthy about our way of life or customs, you have only to
point it out, and we will willingly change.[193] But you must be
able to back up your criticism with the authority of the Gospel.'

Should a response not be forthcoming, turn the discus-
sion to the subject of your constitutions: 'Did our Shepherd[194]

go beyond the limits of any Order or Rule when, with the help of divine grace (and never leaving his cloister) he undertook the spiritual direction of the brethren whom God committed to his care? Did he estrange us from some Order or Rule when, with God's help he made sure that we were united in all matters, permitting no customs among us except love and the service of others?'

Inform us, if you find our ways so reprehensible, if our Shepherd has put us beyond the pale of Order and Rule by forbidding us to return to visit the family and friends we have left in the world, or to drop hints about our poverty when they come visiting us!

Would we be excluded by any Order, or condemned by any Rule because our Shepherd will not suffer us to put up for the night in châteaux, or pass through towns, unless this is completely unavoidable? Has our Shepherd made us unfit for Order or Rule by not giving us leave to attend fairs or market days, not wishing us to become traders or stall-keepers?

Are we disqualified because he forbade us to receive tithes, or rents from great landed estates, which would involve us in endless legal wrangles with layfolk? Has our Shepherd barred us from Order or Rule by banning active ministry, accepting the care of churches, together with the rewards and anxieties that entails? Or by proscribing the keeping of flocks, so that we would be totally free to serve God?

Has he transgressed some point of a Rule by not receiving women into the observance he invented, not permitting them to live in our monasteries or work alongside the brethren?

What Order or Rule has our Shepherd seduced us from by

refusing to hold any bail or bond at the monastery, even if it concerns one of us? He demanded that we really give up the worldly affairs we have renounced, and that we live in our solitudes as though dead to the world, forever on its margins. Are we unfit for Order or Rule because of that?'

So, brothers, with words like this you can answer criticisms of your way of life. But if someone has any suggestions as to how you can keep farther from the world's doings, give your full attention to that! Likewise, ignore any voice—from within or without—counseling more involvement with the world, lest you give it the slightest power over you.

If God's Son would have known a better way than poverty for a human being to gain Heaven, he would surely have chosen that as his path. Love poverty, then, for Jesus Christ chose it as the better part.[195] But do not take what I have said here as an accolade for me or thee. God alone knows how we really stand with him. Yet even if our way of life is not guaranteed holy, at least it is not ambiguous.

See to it that anyone who finds fault with you has your compliments, and humble yourself before them who would praise him. This is what Paul the apostle did.

Let your conviction be firm, that there is no other Rule besides the divine precepts. Anyone who keeps these is a religious; whoever strays from them is living outside the bounds of all Orders and Rules.

ENDNOTES

1 Cf Mt 24:25
2 1 Co 13:5
3 1 Co 4:16; 11:1
4 Ezk 34:14
5 Cf Ps 133:1
6 Rm 10:17
7 Cf 1 Co 12:15 ff
8 Jn 10:7-9
9 Jn 14:6
10 Jn 1:17
11 1 Co 7:33-34; 2 Tm 2:4; Cf Ac
   6:2-4
12 Mt 5:3
13 Jn 15:5
14 Lk 9:23
15   The French used this name
   to refer to the
   Grandmontines. In Latin it
   is 'vir bonus'.
16 Jn 3:30
17 Cf Gn 3:6 ff
18 Ps 104:34
19 Cf Ph 3:20
20 Cf 1 K 1:13
21 Cf Mk 9:41
22 Cf Lk 4:13
23 Jn 1:5
24 Cf Ep 6:16
25 1 Tm 1:15
26 Cf Gn 18; Heb 13:2
27 Cf Jm 3:1
28 Rm 8:8
29 Jn 13:1 ff
30 Mt 18:3
31 Is 9:18-20
32 Mt 15:14

33 Mt 10:39
34 Ph 2:7
35 1 Co 4:7
36 Ps 72:28
37 1 Co 6:15
38 1 Co 2:14
39 Jn 2:24
40 Mt 16:21-23
41 Ps 30:20
42 Ph 3:10
43 Lk 11:34
44 Cf 1 Co 12:27
45 1 Co 11:29
46 2 Co 3:18
47 1 Co 1:9, 10:3; 2 Co 1:8; 1 Th
   3:3
48 Cf Mt 28:8
49 Mk 16:1-8
50 Jn 6:54
51 Cf Heb 2:18
52 1 P 2:20
53 Cf Lk 10:27 a et para
54 Cf Lk 10:27b
55 Mt 25:31-46
56 Cf 2 Co 5:15; Rm 14:7-8
57 Cf Heb 3:7 -13
58 Cf Is 41:24; 59:4
59 Cf. Pss 36:26; 111:5
60 Mt 19:29
61 Cf Rm 8:24 ff
62 Lk 9:25
63 Cf 2 Co 8:9
64 Cf Jn 1:16
65 Cf Lk 23:42 ff
66 Ph 2:8
67 2 Co 4:7

68 Cf Mk 19:7 et para
69 Mt 6:1-6
70 Mk 9:48
71 Mt 18:4
72 Cf Mt 11:29
73 Jn 10:1-2
74 Cf Lk 4:9
75 1 P 5:7
76 Cf Ps 118:103 ff
77 Cf Ps 118:103 ff
78 Lk 10:3
79 Cf Jn 5:23
80 Mt 24:13
81 Mt 11:29
82 Mt 24:36
83 Cf Rv 20:4-6
84 Ps 24:15
85 Cf Mt 11:30; 1 Jn 5:3
86 Mt 7:4
87 Cf 1 Co 9:26; Ga 5:7; Ph 2:16; 2
    Tm 4:7
88 Lk 10:38
89 1 Jn 4:18
90 Mt 5:6
91 Cf Ac 20:35
92 Lk 10:39
93 Lk 10:41
94 Lk 10:42
95 Lk 10:40
96 Cf Ep 1, 12, 14
97 Cf Rm 7:23
98 Lk 10:6
99 Cf Lk 10:6
100 Cf Mt 25:20
101 Cf Gn 11:4
102 Cf Mk 10:18
103 Mt 7:26
104 Cf Mk 4:27
105 Mt 10:26

106 Mt 6:3
107 Ph 1:6
108 1 Co 1:18
109 Lk 16:25
110 Lk 16:25
111 Ep 3:20
112 2 Co 12:7-9
113 Cf Mt 19:22
114 Qo 10:16
115 2 Pt 2:22
116 Cf Jn 13:6-10
117 Rm 12:17-21; Cf Mk 5:44
118 Mt 5:23-24
119 Mt 6:15
120 Jr 31:33
121 Cf Mt 18:8-9
122 Rm 12:19
123 Cf Rm 12:14-19
124 Lk 6:38
125 Cf Heb 4:1-11
126 Cf Ph 1:21-23
127 Cf Lk 6:21
128 Rm 12:20
129 Cf 1 Co 1:18; 2 Co 2:15; 4:3
130 2 Th 2:10; 1 Co 13:3
131 Cf Lk 12:48
132 1 Co 11:27-28
133 Mt 18:23-35
134 Cf Mt 28:20; Heb 8:6
135 Rm 12:1
136 Mt 12:36
137 1 Co 10:13
138 1 Co 10:13, et al
139 Cf Mk 10:40 et paras
140 Cf Ep 1:4
141 1 P 2:4
142 Rm 11:33
143 Jn 12:25
144 Mt 10:9

145 Mt 16:26
146 Ph 1:23
147 1 Co 13:13
148 1 Co 12:32
149 Jn 15:13-15; Sg 5:1, 16
150 Mt 6:19-21
151 Heb 11:16; Pr 3:20
152 Ps 44:11
153 Mt 5:44
154 Mt 5:44
155 Ps 36:27
156 Heb 10:38
157 1 Co 1:9
158 Lk 15:4-6
159 Cf Ws 1:12
160 Ex 12:35-36
161 Dn 3:51
162 Ex 17:8-13
163 Lk 7:36
164 Mt 20-23
165 Mt 5:3
166 Cf Qo 3:1-8
167 1 Co 12:3; 1 Jn 4:19
168 Jn 1:12
169 Ps 32:3; etc.
170 Rv 5:9
171 Jn 13:34
172 Cf Lk 16:8; Ep 5:8; 1 Th 5:5
173 Lk 15:7
174 Ps 23:8, 10
175 Cf Rm 8:28
176 Cf Rm 6:1, 5
177 Cf antiphon 'Salve Regina'.
178 Cf Ep 3:25; 1 P 1:19
179 Cf Ga 4:26
180 Col 3:14; Cf Mt 22:11
181 Col 3:14; Cf Mt 22:11
182 Ps 85:5
183 Mt 22:39

184 Cf Mt 11:39
185 Jm 1:22
186 Dn 13
187 Lk 2:29
188 Ho 2:6
189 Cf Mt 7:24; Mk 4:20
190 Mt 22:37
191 Cf Mk 4:26-29; Jm 5:7; Dn 3:64-67
192 Dn 3:68; Mk 4:28
193 Cf Jn 18:23
194 As in Prologue.
195 Cf Lk 10:42; 1 Co 12:31

CISTERCIAN TEXTS

Bernard of Clairvaux

- Apologia to Abbot William
- Five Books on Consideration: Advice to a Pope
- Homilies in Praise of the Blessed Virgin Mary
- In Praise of the New Knighthood
- Letters of Bernard of Clairvaux / by B.S. James
- Life and Death of Saint Malachy the Irishman
- Love without Measure: Extracts from the Writings of St Bernard / by Paul Dimier
- On Grace and Free Choice
- On Loving God / Analysis by Emero Stiegman
- Parables and Sentences
- Sermons for the Summer Season
- Sermons on Conversion
- Sermons on the Song of Songs I–IV
- The Steps of Humility and Pride

William of Saint Thierry

- The Enigma of Faith
- Exposition on the Epistle to the Romans
- Exposition on the Song of Songs
- The Golden Epistle
- The Mirror of Faith
- The Nature and Dignity of Love
- On Contemplating God: Prayer & Meditations

Aelred of Rievaulx

- Dialogue on the Soul
- Liturgical Sermons, I
- The Mirror of Charity
- Spiritual Friendship
- Treatises I: On Jesus at the Age of Twelve, Rule for a Recluse, The Pastoral Prayer
- Walter Daniel: The Life of Aelred of Rievaulx

Gertrud the Great of Helfta

- Spiritual Exercises
- The Herald of God's Loving-Kindness (Books 1, 2)
- The Herald of God's Loving-Kindness (Book 3)

John of Ford

- Sermons on the Final Verses of the Songs of Songs I–VII

Gilbert of Hoyland

- Sermons on the Songs of Songs I–III
- Treatises, Sermons and Epistles

Other Early Cistercian Writers

- Adam of Perseigne, Letters of
- Alan of Lille: The Art of Preaching
- Amadeus of Lausanne: Homilies in Praise of Blessed Mary
- Baldwin of Ford: The Commendation of Faith
- Baldwin of Ford: Spiritual Tractates I–II
- Geoffrey of Auxerre: On the Apocalypse
- Guerric of Igny: Liturgical Sermons Vol. I & 2
- Helinand of Froidmont: Verses on Death
- Idung of Prüfening: Cistercians and Cluniacs: The Case for Cîteaux
- In the School of Love. An Anthology of Early Cistercian Texts
- Isaac of Stella: Sermons on the Christian Year, I–[II]
- The Life of Beatrice of Nazareth
- Serlo of Wilton & Serlo of Savigny: Seven Unpublished Works
- Stephen of Lexington: Letters from Ireland
- Stephen of Sawley: Treatises
- Three Treatises on Man: A Cistercian

Anthropology

MONASTIC TEXTS

Eastern Monastic Tradition

- Abba Isaiah of Scete: Ascetic Discourses
- Besa: The Life of Shenoute
- Cyril of Scythopolis: Lives of the Monks of Palestine
- Dorotheos of Gaza: Discourses and Sayings
- Evagrius Ponticus: Praktikos and Chapters on Prayer
- Handmaids of the Lord: Lives of Holy Women in Late Antiquity & the Early Middle Ages
- Harlots of the Desert
- John Moschos: The Spiritual Meadow
- Lives of the Desert Fathers
- Lives of Simeon Stylites
- Manjava Skete
- Mena of Nikiou: Isaac of Alexandra & St Macrobius
- The Monastic Rule of Iosif Volotsky (Revised Edition)
- Pachomian Koinonia I–III
- Paphnutius: Histories/Monks of Upper Egypt
- The Sayings of the Desert Fathers
- The Spiritually Beneficial Tales of Paul, Bishop of Monembasia
- Symeon the New Theologian: The Theological and Practical Treatises & The Three Theological Discourses
- Theodoret of Cyrrhus: A History of the

Monks of Syria
- The Syriac Fathers on Prayer and the Spiritual Life

Western Monastic Tradition

- Achard of Saint Victor: Works
- Anselm of Canterbury: Letters I–III / by Walter Fröhlich
- Bede: Commentary…Acts of the Apostles
- Bede: Commentary…Seven Catholic Epistles
- Bede: Homilies on the Gospels I–II
- Bede: Excerpts from the Works of Saint Augustine on the Letters of the Blessed Apostle Paul
- The Celtic Monk
- Gregory the Great: Forty Gospel Homilies
- Life of the Jura Fathers
- The Maxims of Stephen of Muret
- Peter of Celle: Selected Works
- The Letters of Armand Jean-deRancé I–II
- Rule of the Master
- Rule of Saint Augustine

CHRISTIAN SPIRITUALITY

- A Cloud of Witnesses... The Development of Christian Doctrine / by David N. Bell
- The Call of Wild Geese / by Matthew Kelty
- The Cistercian Way / by André Louf
- The Contemplative Path
- Drinking From the Hidden Fountain / by Thomas Spidlík
- Entirely for God / by Elizabeth Isichei
- Eros and Allegory: Medieval Exegesis of the Song of Songs / by Denys Turner
- Fathers Talking / by Aelred Squire
- Friendship and Community / by Brian McGuire
- Grace Can do Moore: Spiritual Accompaniment / by André Louf
- High King of Heaven / by Benedicta Word
- How Far to Follow / by B. Olivera
- The Hermitage Within / by a Monk
- Life of St Mary Magdalene and of Her Sister St Martha / by David Mycoff
- The Luminous Eye / by Sebastian Brock
- Many Mansions / by David N. Bell
- Mercy in Weakness / by André Louf
- The Name of Jesus / by Irénée Hausherr
- No Moment Too Small / by Norvene Vest
- Penthos: The Doctrine of Compunction in the Christian East / by Irénée Hausherr
- Praying the Word / by Enzo Bianchi
- Praying with Benedict / by Korneel Vermeiren
- Russian Mystics / by Sergius Bolshakoff
- Sermons in a Monastery / by Matthew Kelty

- Silent Herald of Unity: The Life of Maria Gabrielle Sagheddu / by Martha Driscoll
- Spiritual Direction in the Early Christian East / by Irénée Hausherr
- The Spirituality of the Christian East / by Thomas Spidlík
- The Spirituality of the Medieval West / by André Vauchez
- The Spiritual World of Isaac the Syrian / by Hilarion Alfeyev
- Tuning In To Grace / by André Louf

MONASTIC STUDIES

- Community and Abbot in the Rule of St Benedict I–II / by Adalbert de Vogüé
- The Hermit Monks of Grandmont / by Carole A. Hutchison
- In the Unity of the Holy Spirit / by Sighard Kleiner
- A Life Pleasing to God: Saint Basil's Monastic Rules / By Augustine Holmes
- Memoirs [of Jean Leclercq]: From Grace to Grace
- Monastic Practices / by Charles Cummings
- The Occupation of Celtic Sites in Ireland / by Geraldine Carville
- Reading St Benedict / by Adalbert de Vogüé
- Rule of St Benedict: A Doctrinal and Spiritual Commentary / by Adalbert de Vogüé
- The Venerable Bede / by Benedicta Ward
- Western Monasticism / by Peter King
- What Nuns Read / by David N. Bell

CISTERCIAN STUDIES

- Aelred of Rievaulx: A Study / by Aelred Squire
- Athirst for God: Spiritual Desire in Bernard of Clairvaux's Sermons on the Song of Songs / by Michael Casey
- Beatrice of Nazareth in Her Context / by Roger De Ganck
- Bernard of Clairvaux: Man, Monk, Mystic / by Michael Casey [tapes and readings]
- Catalogue of Manuscripts in the Obrecht Collection of the Institute of Cistercian Studies / by Anna Kirkwood
- Christ the Way: The Christology of Guerric of Igny / by John Morson
- The Cistercians in Denmark / by Brian McGuire
- The Cistercians in Scandinavia / by James France
- A Difficult Saint / by Brian McGuire
- The Finances of the Cistercian Order in the Fourteenth Century / by Peter King

- Fountains Abbey and Its Benefactors
  / by Joan Wardrop
- A Gathering of Friends: Learning & Spirituality
  in John of Ford / by Costello and Holdsworth
- The Golden Chain...Isaac of Stella /
  byBernard Mc Ginn
- Image and Likeness: Augustinian Spirituality
  of William of St Thierry / by David Bell
- Index of Authors & Works in Cistercian
  Libraries in Great Britain I / by David Bell
- Index of Cistercian Authors and Works in
  Medieval Library Catalogues in Great Britian
  / by David Bell
- The Mystical Theology of St Bernard
  / by Étienne Gilson
- The New Monastery: Texts & Studies on the
  Earliest Cistercians
- Monastic Odyssey / by Marie Kervingant
- Nicolas Cotheret's Annals of Cîteaux
  / by Louis J. Lekai
- Pater Bernhardus: Martin Luther and
  Bernard of Clairvaux / by Franz Posset
- Pathway of Peace / by Charles Dumont
- Rancé and the Trappist Legacy
  / by A. J. Krailsheimer
- A Second Look at Saint Bernard
  / by Jean Leclercq
- The Spiritual Teachings of St Bernard of
  Clairvaux / by John R. Sommerfeldt
- Studies in Medieval Cistercian History
- Three Founders of Cîteaux
  / by Jean-Baptiste Van Damme
- Towards Unification with God (Beatrice of
  Nazareth in Her Context, 2)
- William, Abbot of St Thierry
- Women and St Bernard of Clairvaux
  / by Jean Leclercq

MEDIEVAL RELIGIOUS WOMEN

A Sub-series edited by
Lillian Thomas Shank and John A. Nichols
- Distant Echoes
- Hidden Springs: Cistercian Monastic Women
  (2 volumes)
- Peace Weavers

CARTHUSIAN TRADITION

- The Call of Silent Love / by A Carthusian
- The Freedom of Obedience / by A Carthusian
- From Advent to Pentecost / by A Carthusian
- Guigo II: The Ladder of Monks & Twelve
  Meditations / by E. Colledge & J. Walsh
- Halfway to Heaven / by R.B. Lockhart
- Interior Prayer / by A Carthusian

- Meditations of Guigo I / by A. Gordon Mursall
- The Prayer of Love and Silence / by A Carthusian
- Poor, Therefore Rich / by A Carthusian
- They Speak by Silences / by A Carthusian
- The Way of Silent Love (A Carthusian Miscellany)
- Where Silence is Praise / by A Carthusian
- The Wound of Love (A Carthusian Miscellany)

CISTERCIAN ART, ARCHITECTURE & MUSIC

- Cistercian Abbeys of Britain
- Cistercian Europe / by Terryl N. Kinder
- Cistercians in Medieval Art / by James France
- Studies in Medieval Art and Architecture
  / edited by Meredith Parsons Lillich
  (Volumes II–V are now available)
- Stones Laid Before the Lord
  / by Anselme Dimier
- Treasures Old and New: Nine Centuries of
  Cistercian Music (compact disc and cassette)

THOMAS MERTON

- The Climate of Monastic Prayer / by T. Merton
- Legacy of Thomas Merton / by P. Hart
- Message of Thomas Merton / by P. Hart
- Monastic Journey of Thomas Merton
  / by Patrick Hart
- Thomas Merton/Monk / by P. Hart
- Thomas Merton on St Bernard
- Toward an Integrated Humanity
  / edited by M. Basil Pennington

CISTERCIAN LITURGICAL DOCUMENTS SERIES

- Cistercian Liturgical Documents Series
  / edited by Chrysogonus Waddell, ocso
- Hymn Collection from the...Paraclete
- The Paraclete Statutes:: Institutiones nostrae
- Molesme Summer-Season Breviary (4 vol.)
- Old French Ordinary & Breviary of the
  Abbey of the Paraclete (2 volumes)
- Twelfth-century Cistercian Hymnal (2 vol.)
- The Twelfth-century Cistercian Psalter
- Two Early Cistercian Libelli Missarum

FESTSCHRIFTS

- Bernardus Magister...Nonacentenary of the Birth of St Bernard
- The Joy of Learning & the Love of God: Essays in Honor of Jean Leclercq
- Praise no Less Than Charity in honor of C. Waddell
- Studiosorum Speculumin honor of Louis J. Lekai
- Truth As Gift... in honor of J. Sommerfeldt

BUSINESS INFORMATION

Editorial Offices & Customer Service

- Cistercian Publications
  WMU Station, 1903 West Michigan Avenue
  Kalamazoo, Michigan 49008-5415   USA

  Telephone 616 387 8920
  Fax   616 387 8390
  e-mail   cistpub@wmich.edu

Please Note: As of 13 July 2002 the 616 area code becomes 269

Canada

- Novalis
  49 Front Street East, Second Floor
  Toronto, Ontario M5E 1B3   CANADA

  Telephone 1 800 204 4140
  Fax   416 363 9409

U.K.

- Cistercian Publications UK
  Mount Saint Bernard Abbey
  Coalville, Leicestershire LE67 5UL   UK

- UK Customer Service & Book Orders
  Cistercian Publications
  97 Loughborough Road
  Thringstone, Coalville
  Leicestershire LE67 8LQ   UK

  Telephone 01530 45 27 24
  Fax   01530 45 02 10
  e-mail   MsbcistP@aol.com

Website

- www.spencerabbey.org/cistpub

Trade Accounts & Credit Applications

- Cistercian Publications / Accounting
  6219 West Kistler Road
  Ludington, Michigan 49431   USA

  Fax   231 843 8919

Cistercian Publications is a non-profit corporation. Its publishing program is restricted to monastic texts in translation and books on the monastic tradition.
A complete catalogue of texts in translation and studies on early, medieval, and modern monasticism is available, free of charge, from any of the addresses above.